Socio-Psycho Assessment of Suicide

About the Authors

Dr. Swati Akshay Sachdeva, is Associate Professor, Department of Sociology, Sikkim University, India. Her areas of specialization are Gender studies, Cultural Studies, Eastern Himalayas and refugee studies. She has been working in the field of mental health for more than a decade, closely analysing and tracking the phenomenon of suicide for many years and is an advisor with the main steering committee, of the Government of Sikkim on the issue and has been a collaborator on a Fulbright project on the issue. She has published and presented at conferences and represented India in the 'High level political forum, 2018 at the United Nations. She is also a counsellor and a motivational speaker.

Yumnam Surjyajeevan, is Research Scholar in Department of Sociology, Sikkim University, India. His area of specialisation are ethnic identity issues, particularly in the North Eastern Region of India. However, his area of interest widely varies, ranging from ethnic politics, identity issues of refugees, development studies, social medicine, gender and health, youth and unemployment. He also has worked on various state sponsored studies related to demand of Scheduled Tribe status, social impact assessment, social issues revolving around suicide.

Socio-Psycho Assessment of Suicide

Swati A. Sachdeva
Yumnam Surjyajeevan

CONCEPT PUBLISHING COMPANY PVT. LTD.
NEW DELHI-110059

ISBN-13: 978-93-88937-63-4

First Published 2020

Published and Printed by

Concept Since 1974

Concept Publishing Company Pvt. Ltd.
A/15-16, Commercial Block, Mohan Garden,
New Delhi-110059 (INDIA)
T: 91 11 25351460, 91 11 25351794
E: publishing@conceptpub.com; *W*: www.conceptpub.com

Cataloging in Publication Data--Courtesy: D.K. Agencies (P) Ltd. <docinfo@dkagencies.com>

Sachdeva, Swati A., author.
Socio-psycho assessment of suicide / Swati A. Sachdeva, Yumnam Surjyajeevan.
pages cm
Includes bibliographical references and index.
ISBN 9789388937634

1. Suicide—India—Sikkim—Psychological aspects. 2. Suicide—Social aspects—India—Sikkim. 3. Suicidal behavior—India—Sikkim. I. Surjyajeevan, Yumnam, author. II. Title.

LCC HV6548.I52S55 2020 | DDC 362.280954167 23

Preface

Sikkim as a state of India, has opened-up to economic development in recent years with investment in infrastructure and communication technology resulting in rapid social change, which have a destabilizing impact on the society. It was a harmonious agriculturally based religious society based on social cohesiveness and mechanical solidarity. However, development is bringing about social and cultural changes through increasing media exposure to the global consumer economy. Rapid cultural change and erosion of indigenous cultural values and identity through the increasing interconnectedness that globalization brings with it, seems to be at the root of pervasive feelings of stress and anxiety.

Sikkim has the second highest incidence of Suicide in India among the States/UTs, as per the latest NCRB 2015 report. The present book is based on further exhaustive and in-depth study and quantitative statistical analysis of 242 samples (Z) which was sampled out from the original 351 (N) suicide victims and 35 Psycho-autopsies which were collected from the four Districts of Sikkim.

Through the statistical generalisation, it was found that the highest 74.28 per cent of the suicide victims belong to the age group between 16-45 years. District-wise, then highest suicide cases occurred in the South district (34.44%) followed by 32.78 per cent in East district, while the lowest percentage was recorded in North district. The Sikkimese population possessing SSC/COI/*parcha* accounts to 65.56 per cent of the total samples. As per gender representation, more males have committed suicide as compared to women. In terms of settlement pattern, 79.32 per cent of the suicide victims are from the rural population, while only 20.68 per cent constitute urban population. In relation to educational qualification, it was found that majority of the victims were educated up to primary (23.55%), followed by illiterate (19.42%). In terms of monthly income, majority of the deceased were found to be in the income group of less than Rs. 7,500 (48.35%). Among the religious group, suicide cases were found among all major religious groups. Although the Hindus were the highest percentage, it should be understood in terms of their population percentage.

Further, in the correlation analysis between age groups, monthly income and relationship problems, it was found that the specified age group, i.e. 16-45, were the most vulnerable to suicide due to relationship problems which is further correlated with financial issues particularly with those belonging the income range of up to Rs. 15,000 per month.

The study shows that there is a significant relation between suicide and alcohol consumption that is 53.53 per cent of the suicides were of habitual alcoholic whereas, 46.47 per cent were non-alcoholic or social drinkers. There is a positive correlation between unemployment and alcohol consumption (62.5%), that is, unemployed population consuming alcohol are more prone to suicides than those of employed population consuming alcohol.

In correlational analysis of health problems with monthly income, it was observed that the incidence of suicide is highest among the low income group whose monthly income is less than Rs. 7,500 (42.42%), which is followed by (Rs. 15,000-25,000) income range.

Occupation-wise, it was found in the correlation analysis that higher cases of suicides were common among the dropouts who were occupationally engaged in farming (36.63%), followed by housewives (16.28%), unemployed (8.72%) and so forth.

It was observed that suicide in Sikkim is highest among the married individuals constituting 58.51 per cent of the total suicide cases in Sikkim. This is an important aspect of the study as in most of the suicide cases observed around the world are common among the unmarried individuals. Alcoholism and illness were also found which create relationship related problems.

Summing-up both quantitative and qualitative narrative analysis, it can be safely concluded that most of the causal factors of suicides are rooted largely in the social fabric of the society. The changes which are taking place at the larger socio-cultural and economic level results in the emotional breakdown of the individuals at the psychological level which make it difficult for them to cope up with the changes. Although, the subjective experiences vary across individuals, nonetheless, these experiences form a pattern which is shared as inter-subjective experience by many of the victims.

There is a need for short-term and long-term culturally sensitive interventions at many levels. There is also an urgent need to support and strengthen the initiatives that are already under way. The state as an external agency can play a vital role in addressing socio-economic issues that are largely rooted in social structure.

Acknowledgements

This book is the collective effort of the research team based at Sikkim University which was duly funded and sponsored by DESM&E (Department of Economics, Statistics, Monitoring and Evaluation), Government of Sikkim, India. The findings, analysis and policy recommendations are those of the researchers based on their field analysis. The main objective was to understand the sociological and psychological relation to the suicides in Sikkim as the rates are very alarming with respective to the population size and demography of Sikkim.

We are grateful to Prof. T.B. Subba, Honorable Vice Chancellor, Sikkim University for his continued inspirational intellectual advice, guidance and thoughts.

We thank our Funding agency DESM&E. We were privileged to receive the duly assistance to the research team for successfully carrying out the research. We thank and acknowledge the following members from DESM&E: Mrs. Madhu Pradhan (Director), Mrs. Irene O. Chankapa (Director II); Mrs. S.K. Pradhan (Joint Director); Mr. T. Geleg (Additional Director); Mr. Jeevan Tamang (Additional Director) and his team of field officials for their kind contributions in providing us the financial support and guidance.

Particular appreciation is due for Prof. Rashmi Jaipal (Professor Emeritus and Cross Cultural Psychologist, American Psychological Association, UN) and Dr. Sunil Verma (Assistant Professor, Vivekanand College, Delhi University) for their invaluable research inputs and encouragement.

We thank all our colleagues and faculty members—Dr. K. Indira, Mr. Shankar N. Bagh, Ms. Sona Rai and Binod Bhattarai (all are Assistant Professors, Department of Sociology, School of Social Sciences, Sikkim University) for their moral support and encouragement.

The most important contribution has come from Dr. Sandhya Thapa, Associate Professor, Department of Sociology, School of Social Sciences, Sikkim University, for framing of questionnaires, conceptualizing the structural framework and providing detailed inputs to the book.

We are especially thankful to all our respondents from the deceased families, medical doctors, NGOs, teachers, faculties and principals of various schools, panchayats, psychiatrists, counsellors and all other members directly or indirectly involved for their most valuable feedback during the group discussions and survey. Without their kind help and support, this book would have not been possible. Death is always a trauma for family and relatives and to help us through answering the questionnaire and participating in open group discussions require great amount of courage and we are ever thankful and indebted to all our contributors for their help.

We acknowledge and thank our seven field surveyors—Tenzee, Rinchen, Neha, Chutim, Sanjay, Shanti and Nepash for collecting the data from the difficult terrain of Sikkim in harsh climatic conditions. They did a tremendous job in collecting the data from the information available as per the database of DESM&E. It is due to their hard work we achieved such valuable data for preparing this report.

To ensure accuracy and clarity, the statistical analysis has benefited from the discussions of statistical issues duly helped from our Data Analysis and Technical Support members. We thank Mr. Ishfaq Nabi Najar and Mr. Sayak Das (Ph.D. Scholars, Department of Microbiology, School of Life Sciences, Sikkim University) for their kind patience and technical support on this project.

The consultations, discussions and the great amount of home work held during the preparation of the book relied on the research team and generous support of many institutions and individuals.

We are grateful to our team for the highly professional editing and formatting of questionnaires, on-field survey, data collection, data entry, data compilation and data analysis which finally helped us in writing this book.

On a personal note, we acknowledge and express our gratitude to Sikkim University for providing us the platform for research which we hope shall help in the development of Sikkim.

Swati A. Sachdeva
Yumnam Surjyajeevan

Contents

List of Tables and Figures

List of Tables

List of Figures

1

Introduction

Durkheim in his 1897 book *Le suicide* wrote "the most varied and even the most contradictory events of life may equally serve as pretexts for suicide", suggesting the inability to pin down the social causality of suicide (Durkheim, 1979 [1897]: 298). For instance, "One man kills himself in the midst of affluence, another in the lap of poverty; one was unhappy in his home, and another had just ended by divorce a marriage which was making him unhappy. In one case a soldier ends his life after having been punished for an offense he did not commit; in another, a criminal whose crime has remained unpunished kills himself" (*ibid.* 297-8). However, from the studies of more than 26 thousand suicide cases in Europe, he theorised the causal factor of suicide to be social in nature and origin focused particularly on the level of integration and regulations played by various social undercurrents of the time. Prior to Durkheim's study of suicide, there had been the tendency of taking suicide as an individualised personal problem and not as a social issue (sadly, even now people tend to take suicide as a case of mental health). In this sense the society has failed to recognise and differentiate the personal problems to that of social issue as highlighted by Mills in *Sociological Imagination.* By sociological imagination, Mills refers to the ability or 'quality of mind' which is "essential to grasp the interplay of man and society, of biography and history, of self and world" (Mills, 2000 [1959]: 4). The argument Mills gave is that most of the social aspects of our personal lives are determined by the social structure, yet we fail to recognise the structurally conditioned and detrimental problems. For instance, in a hilly region like Sikkim or Darjeeling, if few households, let's say 5 in 1,000, are facing water issues in their household then it is a personal problem due to various reasons known to them; however, if out of these 1,000 households 40 to 50 per cent households are facing the crisis related to water problem, then, it is no longer a personal problem but rather a serious social issue which the State should address. Therefore, to Mills, "sociological imagination enables us to grasp history and biography and the relations between the two within society" (*ibid.*: 6).

The next question is, that is suicide still a personal problem restricted to psychological domain of humans' reasoning or is it socially rooted in the structural conditioning? If we observe the rate of suicide committed throughout the world every year, as per WHO (2016) suicide record, over 8,00,000 people die every year due to suicide, which is the second highest cause of death among the age group of 15 to 29 years old, suicide cannot be confined to the realm of psychological explanation alone, in fact, as Durkheim theorised, it has to do with the structural conditioning of the social system. The World Health Organisation (WHO) manual on the prevention of suicide pointed that "social, psychological, cultural and other factors can lead a person to suicidal behaviour"; the insignia is further directed toward the social causes of suicide, as suicides frequently occur in "low- and middle-income countries where resources and services, if they do exist, are often scarce and limited for early identification, treatment and support of people in need" (WHO, 2016: 3).

India, being one of the low-income countries, more than one lakh people (1,31,666) lost their lives by committing suicide during the year 2014, which has increased to 1,33,623 in 2015. As per the National Crime Record Bureau (NCRB) 2014 and 2015 report, the figurative decadal increment of suicide rate during 2004-2014 is 15.8 per cent, whereas the rate is 17.3 per cent in 2005-2015. However, taking account of the decadal population growth during the period, which is 14.6 per cent, the net decadal increment in the incidence of suicide in India is 1.2 per cent. An increase in incidences of suicides was reported each year up to 2011 (*Source*: Registrar General of India, 2012). During the year 2012, Tamil Nadu has reported the highest number of suicides (16,927) accounting for 12.5 per cent of total suicides followed by Maharashtra (16,112), West Bengal (14,957), Andhra Pradesh (14,238) and Karnataka (12,753) accounting for 11.9 per cent, 11.0 per cent, 10.5 per cent and 9.4 per cent respectively of the total suicides in the country. These 5 States together accounted for 55.3 per cent of the total suicides reported in the country. The remaining 44.7 per cent suicides were reported in the rest of 23 States and 7 UTs. Uttar Pradesh, the most populous state (16.9% share of population) has reported comparatively lower percentage of suicidal deaths, accounting for only 3.3 per cent of the total suicides reported in the country. All the five States, viz. Tamil Nadu, West Bengal, Andhra Pradesh, Maharashtra and Karnataka have registered consistently higher number of suicidal deaths during the last few years. These States have accounted for about 10 per cent or more of the total suicides reported in the country during 2009 to 2011. Tamil Nadu reported the highest number of suicidal deaths in 2010 and 2012, third highest in 2011 accounting for 12.3 per cent, 11.8 and 12.5 per cent respectively of total such deaths in the country.

However, during 2014, the highest incidents of suicides occurred in Maharashtra (16,307) followed by Tamil Nadu (16,122), West Bengal (14,310), Karnataka (10,945) and Telangana (9,623) accounting for 12.4 per cent, 12.2 per cent, 10.9 per cent, 8.3 per cent and 7.3 per cent respectively of total suicides reported in the country. Cumulatively, 51.1 per cent of the total suicides reported in the country are accounted in these five States, the remaining 48.9 per cent incidents of suicide reported are disproportionately distributed among the 24 States and 7 Union Territories (UTs) (NCRB, 2014). Among the UTs, Delhi has reported the highest cases of suicide (2,095) followed by Puducherry (644); however, the aggregated figure of the 7 UTs accounted only 2.4 per cent of the total suicide incidents in the country in 2014.

Figure 1.1 on page 4, presents a total different scenario of the incidents of suicide in India. The annual escalation in the number of incidents of suicides in India in 2014 over 2013 as given in the NCRB 2014 report, there has been a significant increase in the state of Manipur that is highest in the country with an annual increment of 35.1 per cent followed by Sikkim (32.6%), Mizoram (22.1%), Puducherry (17.9%) and Himachal Pradesh (16.2%). In terms of decrease, Nagaland has reported an overall decrease of 64.9 per cent followed by Andhra Pradesh (58.2%) and Uttarakhand (43.3%). Further, if we try to see the rate of suicides in India and the variation across the 29 States and 7 UTs as presented in Figure 1.2, then, yet again this presents itself a new dimension in the incidents of suicides scenario in the country.

Rate of suicides is the number of suicides per one lakh population. From this perspective, the UT of Puducherry (40.4%) has highest rate of suicides in India during the period of 2014; however, if we look among the States of India then, Sikkim, the second smallest

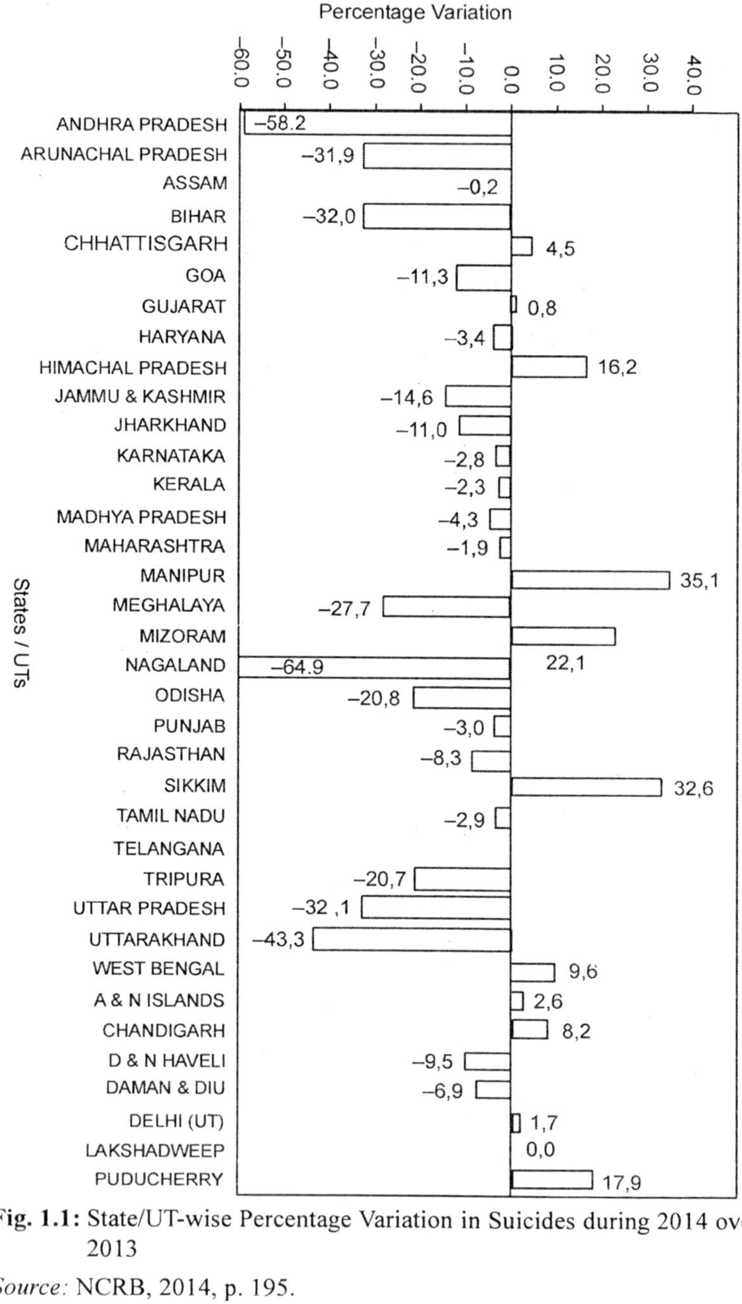

Fig. 1.1: State/UT-wise Percentage Variation in Suicides during 2014 over 2013

Source: NCRB, 2014, p. 195.

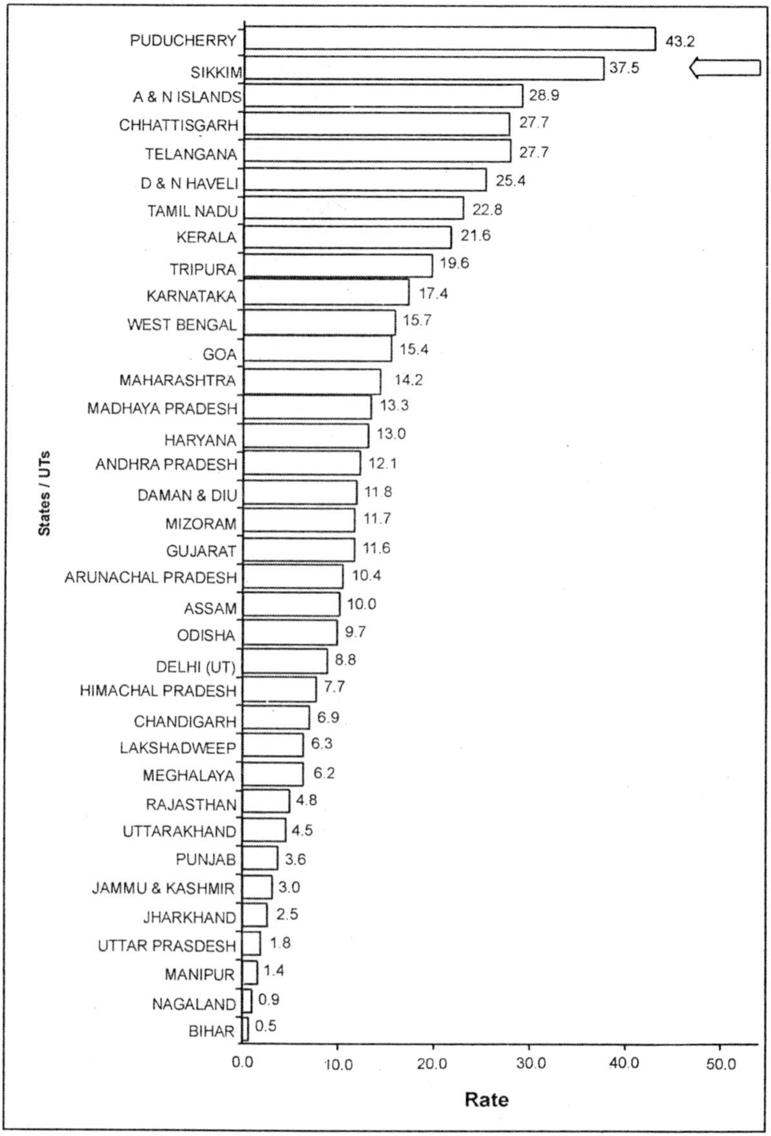

Fig. 1.2: Rate of Suicides in States/UTs during 2015

Source: NCRB, 2014.

State of India, recorded highest suicide incidents of 38.4 per cent among the States of India followed by Telangana (26.5%), Kerala (23.9%), Tamil Nadu (23.4%). The third highest rate of suicides occurred in the UT of Andaman & Nicobar Islands with 28.9 per cent. These figures are way above the national rate of suicides average of 10.6 per cent.

Table 1.1: States/UTs with Higher Suicide Rate during 2012 to 2015

YEARS							
2012		*2013*		*2014*		*2015*	
States/UTs	*Suicide Rate*	*States/ UTs*	*Suicide Rate*	*States/ UTs*	*Suicide Rate*	*States/ UTs*	*Suicide Rate*
Puducherry	36.8	Puducherry	35.6	Puducherry	40.4	Puducherry	43.2
Sikkim	29.1	Sikkim	29.3	Sikkim	38.4	Sikkim	37.5
Tamil Nadu	24.9	A & N Islands	28.8	A & N Islands	28.9	A & N Islands	28.5
Kerala	24.3	Tripura	25.9	Telangana	26.5	Chhattisgarh	27.7
A & N Islands	23.6	Kerala	24.6	Kerala	23.9	Telangana	27.7
National Average	11.2	National Average	11.0	National Average	10.6	National Average	10.6

Source: NCRB 2014 & 2015.

From the above Table 1.1, we can observe the top five most incidents of suicide occurring States/UTs in the last three years suicide rate of the country (2012-2014). The table shows that both Puducherry and Sikkim have consistently maintained its relative position in the list, being highest and second highest rate of suicide incidence occurring States/UTs respectively in last three years. In 2013 the rate of suicides in Puducherry decreased by 1.2 per cent over 2012, so to say, though Puducherry remained the highest in the rate of suicides in the country, nonetheless it keeps on fluctuating. However, in the case of Sikkim, it seems that over the years, the incidence of suicide is gradually increasing, which is a matter of grave concern, except in 2015 it has slightly come down. So it can be advocated, that the problem of suicide is no longer a personal problem in Sikkim, rather a social issue that requires immediate attention and action both from the state as well as from the civil society.

Suicide Scenario in Sikkim

As highlighted above, Sikkim has the second highest incidence of

Suicide in India among the States/UTs, as shown in Table 1.1. As per the latest NCRB 2015 report, the annual suicide rate of Sikkim is 37.5 per cent in 2015, which has come down by 0.9 per cent as compared to 2014 suicide rate (38.4%). In a 10-year retrospective study conducted by Chettri *et al.* (2016), found that the incidence of suicide in Sikkim is highest among the age group of 21-30 (24.4%) followed by the age group of 11-20 and 31-40 accounting 20.9 per cent and 17.3 per cent respectively. It is noted that 62.6 per cent of the suicides in Sikkim occurred among the age group of 11-40, which is a matter of grave concern, as in any society this age group has been considered as the most productive and reproductive age group representing the youth of the society.

Table 1.2: 13 Years' Suicide Scenario in Sikkim (2005-2017)

Year	*Sex*				*Total No.*
	Male		*Female*		
2005	68	62.39	41	37.61	109
2006	71	61.74	44	38.26	115
2007	83	68.03	39	31.97	122
2008	120	66.30	61	33.70	181
2009	90	60.81	58	39.19	148
2010	115	70.12	49	29.88	164
2011	86	58.90	60	41.10	146
2012	119	67.61	57	32.39	176
2013	125	67.93	59	32.07	184
2014	116	64.80	63	35.20	179
2015	154	70.32	65	29.68	219
2016	127	67.20	62	32.80	189
2017	156	76.09	49	23.90	205
Total	**1,430**	**66.91**	**707**	**33.08**	**2,137**
Average	**110**	**66**	**54**	**34**	**164**

Source: Field Data collected from Police Department.

Now, if we observe Table 1.2 and Figure 1.3 we can see that on an average 164 suicides are committed annually in Sikkim, of which 110 are male and 54 female. The year 2008 marked the highest jump in the suicide number as compared to previous year, which was 48.36 per cent increase in the number of suicide over 2007. Again in 2015, the number of suicides increased by 22.35 per cent over 2014. 2017 was the year where the number of male suicide was highest amounting 76.09 per cent, while the year 2011 recorded highest in the number

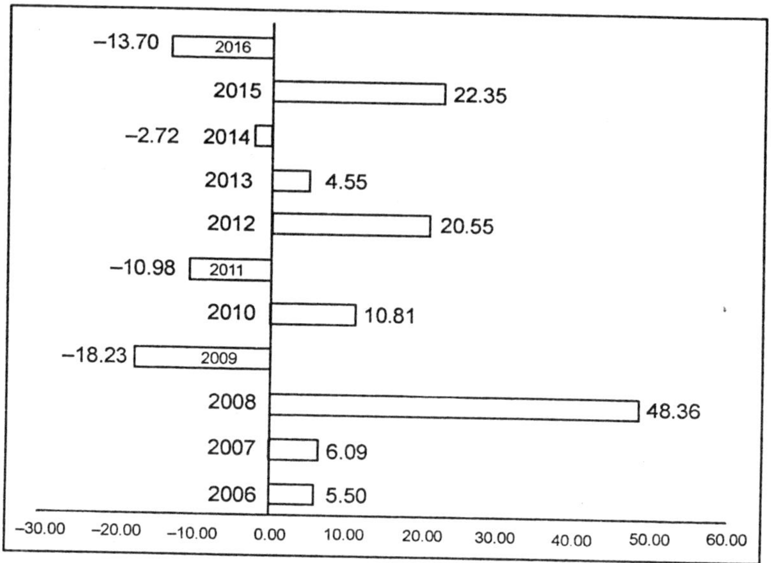

Fig. 1.3: Annual variation in suicide rate over the preceding years (2005-2017)

Source: Field Data collected from Police Department.

of suicide among females (41.10%). The year 2017 has again marked an increase of 8.46 per cent over the previous year.

Table 1.3: District and sex-wise recorded suicide cases in 2013-2015

Districts	2013			2014			2015			Grand Total	Percentage
	Male	Female	Total	Male	Female	Total	Male	Female	Total		
North	4	1	5	1	5	6	4	1	5	16	3.06
West	25	8	33	24	11	35	23	9	32	100	19.12
South	25	19	44	23	19	42	30	12	42	128	24.47
East	58	23	81	42	21	63	49	24	73	217	41.49
State	112	51	163	90	56	146	106	46	152	461	88.15
Outside State/ Address not Stated	11	7	18	10	4	14	18	12	30	62	11.85
Total	123	58	181	100	60	160	124	58	182	523	100.00

Source: Field Data collected from Police Department.

The district-wise number of suicides presented in Table 1.3 shows that East district has higher concentration of the suicide cases (41.49%), while North has least number of suicide cases (3.06%), while those from outside Sikkim (address not stated) constitute 11.85 per cent of the suicide victims. However, this figure should not be taken literally since it needs to compared with to the population ratio of each districts. As per 2011 Census, the population of Sikkim is 6,10,577, of which 7.16 per cent are in the North district, 22.35 per cent in West district, 24.05 per cent in South district and the highest concentration in the East district with 46.45 per cent (Census, 2011). Therefore, if we contrast the number of suicide with that of the population ratio of each district than we can conclude that South district has higher number of suicide cases, as the population percentage of the district is 24.05 per cent but the suicide occurrence is 24.47 per cent.

Table 1.4: Age and sex-wise suicide cases in 2013-2015

Age Range	*2013*			*2014*			*2015*			*Grand Total*	*Percentage*
	Male	Female	Total	Male	Female	Total	Male	Female	Total		
0-15	7	7	14	4	8	12	5	5	10	36	6.88
16-30	41	26	67	45	23	68	50	22	72	207	39.58
31-45	30	9	39	23	13	36	35	20	55	130	24.86
46-60	12	6	18	11	6	17	12	5	17	52	9.94
61<	6	2	8	6	2	8	9	1	10	26	4.97
Age not stated	27	8	35	11	8	19	13	5	18	72	13.77
Total	123	58	181	100	60	160	124	58	182	523	100.00

Source: Field Data collected from Police Department.

Table 1.4 shows the age and sex-wise distribution of the suicide cases occurred during 2013 to 2015. The age group between 16-30 has highest occurrence of suicide, constituting 39.58 per cent of the suicide cases, whereas the least number of occurrence is observable between the age group of 61 and above 4.97 per cent. Therefore, the high rate of risk group is between the age group of 16-30.

Before going further into the detailed scenario of suicide in the State, it is important to clarify some of the conceptual issues and concerns in the study of suicide in general. The study has always been under the shadow of psychology staying far away from the domain of sociological understanding, particularly in the theorisation of the causality of suicide and in terms of an amicable solution of the problem in Sikkim. Therefore, this study aims at resolving the issues of conceptual and methodological clarification, and to develop psycho-sociological theorisation of the social problem of suicide in Sikkim though various hypothetical postulates that will be examined through statistical analysis. To address all these issues, one needs to fall back to the available literatures on the issue.

Suicide in History

Suicide or the intentional act of killing oneself has always been part of the human society and its civilisation. Causes and rates of suicide varied from culture to culture and it is considered as a sin in many religions and crime in some jurisdictions. For instance, not long ago in India, attempted suicide was criminalised under section 309 of Indian Penal Code (IPC). However, with the passing of *Mental Healthcare Bill* on 27th of March, 2017 in the Lower House of the Parliament, any attempted suicide was decriminalized. In relation to attempted suicide, the Bill made a clause stating, "not withstanding anything contained in section 309 of the Indian Penal Code, any person who attempts to commit suicide shall be presumed, unless proved otherwise, to have severe stress and shall not be tried and punished under the said Code."[1] Religiously speaking, many religions such Buddhism, Confucianism, Shintoism accepted suicide and euthanasia in situations of incurable illness and considered it as an honourable way to exit certain shameful or hopeless situations. Among the Hindus, the practice of *Sati*—where women set themselves on fire in the funeral pyre of their dead husband was accepted traditionally in India, till recently.[2] Similarly, the Jews community are also in practice of suicides mainly to escape the consequences of shame, deterioration of status and honour or capture related to military and political defeat. Similar causes are attributed to Roman times in Greek and Rome. Suicide was also observed among soldiers when the leader was killed in a battle (Morgan, 1979). In Japan, ritualistic suicide by disembowelment known as *'Hara Kiri'* was a customary practice among the warriors after their defeat, as an offshoot of this practice, the *Kamikaze* form of suicide during the Second World War was very common. In Durkheimian frame of analysis, this form of suicide is referred as altruistic suicide, which was also prevalent among the military officers in Nineteenth century Europe to avoid dishonour (Durkheim, 1979 [1897]).

Nonetheless, contradictorily, suicide is also condemned severely in several religions. For instant among, the Sikhs, as part of their theological belief, life is a special gift of God and should be given due respect. For such reason, the Sikh Gurus rejected suicide as an interference in God's plan. Suffering, they said, was part of the *karma*, and human beings should not only accept it without complaint but also to make the best of the situation that *karma* has given them. In ancient Israel suicide was a taboo. Because God had made the world, it was supposed to be good (the world) and therefore, one needs to protect it rather wasting it by attempting suicide. In Christianity, suicide is considered a sin, and hold the belief that those who commit suicide will not enter the gate of heaven. St. Augustine (A.D. 354-430) pronounced it as a 'greater sin'.

Suicide: The Psycho-Social Interplay

Oxford English Dictionary states that the word *Suicidium* (suicide) derived by combining two Latin words, *Sui* (on oneself) and the verb *Cidium* (an act of killing or slaying), referring to the 'act of killing oneself'. For Durkheim (1979) "Suicide is applied to all cases of death resulting directly or indirectly from a positive or negative act of the victim himself, which he knows will produce this result" (Durkheim, 1979 [1897]: 44). In English, the word suicide is argued to have first used in 1651, but Alfred Alvarez (1972) reported that it appeared in Sir Thomas Browne's *Religio Medici* in 1642. For Shneidman (1996), "Suicide is a conscious act of self-induced annihilation, where an individual perceives suicide as the best solution for the problem at hand".

Koskay *et al.* (1990) observed that suicidal behaviour can be interpreted as a manifestation of distress associated with loss or abandonment, a release from despair, an expression of hostility or revenge, and an appeal for help, a wish to test fate, a response to the disordered thinking of a psychotic illness or drug intoxication. Though many people may be in a similar situation, but only some people commit suicide. Suicide, in general, is the outcome of a complex interplay of etiological factors which are psychological, biological, and social in origin (Mann *et al.*, 2005). From the two arguments above, it becomes notional that suicide is not just psychological or social factor alone, but rather interplay of these two factors resulting in the final act of suicide.

According to the NCRB 2014 report, one of the main cause of suicide in India is 'Other Family Problems' accounting 21.7 per cent, which can be argued that family has become a site of contestation and there is tremendous stress in the relation among the family members. This argument can be validated by the rising number of suicide cases related to this issue; as in the NCRB 2015 report, indicates that 'Family Problems' has contributed 27.6 per cent in the total number of suicide cases in India. Besides the 'Family Problems' as the major cause of suicide, other causes of suicide in India as per the report are 'Illness' which accounted for 18 per cent in 2014 which has come down to 15.8 per cent in 2015. This aspect of suicide highlights the lacuna in health accessibility scenario of India. Bankruptcy/Indebtedness has also increased from 1.8 per cent to 3.3 per cent to; in relation to youth—'Failure in Examination', 'Unemployment', and 'Love Affairs' have increased from 1.8 per cent to 2.0 per cent, 1.7 per cent to 2.0 per cent, and 3.2 per cent to 3.3 per cent respectively, as shown in Table 1.5.

Table 1.5: Comparison between 2014 and 2015 of the causes of suicide

Causes	*2014 Report*	*2015 Report*
Family Problems	21.7%	27.6%
Illness	18%	15.8%
Marriage Related Issues	5.1%	4.8%
Love Affairs	3.2%	3.3%
Drug Abuse/Addiction	2.8%	2.7%
Bankruptcy/Indebtedness	1.8%	3.3%
Failure in Examination	1.8%	2.0%
Unemployment	1.7%	2.0%
Poverty	1.3%	1.3%
Property Dispute	0.8%	1.9%
Other Causes	33.2%	26.2%
Causes Not Known	12.4%	12.1%

Source: NCRB 2014 and 2015 report.

Further, if we look at the data related to professionals as per the 2015 NCRB report, 'House Wives' constitute 16.7 per cent of total suicide victims; however, if we calculate the figure within the female victims then it constitutes 53.0 per cent. Deductively generalising, we can argue that the brunt of 'Family Problems' which is the highest reported suicide case in India, is being suffered by the 'House Wives'. This is followed by Daily Wage Earner (17.8%), Self-Employed Persons (9.1%), Unemployed Persons (8.2%), Professionals/Salaried Persons (7.9%), Students (6.7%), and Retired Persons (0.8%).

Perspectives on Suicide

Broadly speaking, three ways have been formulated in comprehending the phenomena of suicide, as existing literatures are concerned, which are sociology, psychiatry, and biology. Sociological perspective of suicide, particularly following Durkheimian approach, looks at the patterns of integration of individual with groups in society and the structural constrains and regulatory mechanism that influence the suicide rates. While, the Psychological perspective emphasizes more on personality and emotional disorders as cause of suicide. The Biological view sees physical disorders, often a biochemical imbalance, as the cause of suicide. Shneidman (1993), psychological, psychiatric and sociological perspectives have emphasized on different causes of suicide as shown in Table 1.3. These factors overlap but also are interdependent on each other. For instance, sociological factors such as unemployment, and economic crisis may lead to psychological feelings of low self-esteem, isolation and feelings of worthlessness and it may result in psychiatric disorders like depression and schizophrenia. These three streams are related with one another as individual's relations with group will influence the individual psychologically and it may result in psychiatric disorders, which may lead to suicide (Fig. 1.4).

However, for the present study of suicide in Sikkim, the psychological and sociological approaches are given more importance. Most of the psychiatric perspective is concerned with mental health issues and are treated more or less as a disease/illness. For the said reason, the study will not go to the realm of psychiatric issues. However, as there is interplay between the psychological and social well-being of an individual, the study will theoretically explore the psychological and sociological perspectives on suicide.

Psychological Perspective	*Psychiatric Perspective*	*Sociological Perspective*
Low Self-Esteem	Depression	Unemployment Rates
Depression		Disturbed Marital Status
Loss and Grief	Schizophrenia	Influence of Religion
Disturbed Relationships		Economic Crises
Alienation	Neurobiological Factors	Migration and Ethnicity
Isolation		Societal Expectations
Feelings of Worthlessness	Personality Disorders (Borderline, Anti-social)	Societal Values
Guilt and Shame		Demographic (Rural & Urban)
Inappropriate Coping Skills		
Disturbed Family Back-ground	Substance Abuse (Alcoholism, Drug)	
Coping with Stress and Crisis		Availability of the Means

Fig. 1.4: Comparison of psychological, psychiatric and sociological perspective

Psychological Perspective

Many psychodynamic theorists believe that suicide results primarily from depression and unexpressed anger at others which is redirected inward towards oneself. This theory was first stated by Wilhelm Stekel (1910), in a meeting in Vienna when he proclaimed that "no one kills himself who has not wanted to kill another or at least wished the death of another" (Shneidman, 1979). Freud (1920) identified instinct, as drives that which are innate, universal and constantly felt and these instincts are two types: life instinct (Eros) and death instinct (Thanatos). In the extreme emotional distress the death instinct dominates and becomes powerful over life instinct and these extreme emotional distresses are known as depression, i.e. self-accusation and feeling of worthlessness. Freudian theory sees depression and suicidal act resulting from withdrawal from society and represent hostile impulse directed towards others (Marwaha, 2005). According to Futterman (1961) these two instincts are not separate and could not really function independently of each other, but they always co-exist in variable amounts. Menninger (1938) in his work extended the concept of death instinct and generated a hypothesis that three elements exist in constantly shifting patterns in all self-destructive behaviour, i.e. the wish to kill, the wish to be killed, and the wish to die.

Supporting Freudian view, researchers have found close ties between childhood experiences and later suicidal behaviours (Paykel 1991). Bouckoms and Streiner (1982) studies of 200 family histories found that suicide attempters were more likely to occur to those individuals who have lost a parent during their childhood than the non-suicidal control subjects. Common forms of feeling of loss by individuals were found to be related to death of father and divorce of the parents experienced during their formative years or late adolescence. Shneidman (1993) suggests that the key to suicide is 'psych-ache'—a feeling of psychological pain, tension, and suffering that makes life intolerable. Suicide attempts may also be preceded by shifts in patterns of thinking. Individuals may become preoccupied with their problems, loss perspective, and see suicide as the only effective solution to their difficulties. They develop a sense of hopelessness—a pessimistic belief that their present conditions, circumstances, problems or mood will not change (Klingman and Hochdorf, 1993).

According to hopelessness theory (Abramson *et al.*, 1989) "the expectation that highly desired outcomes will not occur or that highly aversive outcomes will occur and that there is nothing one can do to change this situation." Thus, a kind of "hopelessness depression" sets in when it seems to be no prospect to get either what one really wants or to avoid one really does not want. As part of this theory, negative events can serve as "occasion setters" for people to become hopeless, and there is a "cognitive vulnerability" depressive thinking that accompanies the stress of such negative life events. The self-discrepancy theory (Higgins, 1987) draws on three different concepts of the self: the actual self, as one sees oneself; the ought self, which is the self-one thinks one ought to be; and the ideal self, which is the self-one would most likely to be. The theory for these three concepts states that "individuals are motivated to achieve a state in which there is consistency between the self-concept and these self-evaluative standards". Those "who possess discrepancies between their actual and ideal selves are relatively more prone to developing depression while those who possess discrepancies between their actual and ought selves are relatively more prone to developing anxiety. Simply, this theory has shown a strong correlation between negative evaluation of the self and suicidality. The Escape theory (Baumeister, 1990) states, "Self-destructive behaviours can be explained in terms of motivation to escape from aversive self-awareness and negative effect", an acute negative experience, calamity, or stressor can point up the large discrepancy that exists between what one wants or expects and what actually occurs and where what are often "unrealistically high expectations or standards" can be abruptly dashed. Then, "when setbacks or discrepancies occur, individuals can either hold external factors responsible and absolve themselves of responsibility, or blame themselves and take on responsibility for the failure." Negative emotions, such as depression, anxiety, and anger, can arise from the resulting aversive, negative self-awareness.

Finally, Psychologists viewed suicide, as an intensely personal act of self-destruction and highlighted the role of the psychopathic states like depression and feeling of hopelessness and helplessness in explaining suicides. It emphasizes and examines the individual, and the conflicts within a particular mind leading to self-destructive behaviour. Psychologists emphasize on unbearable and unendurable pain as a cause of suicide but they did not explain the source of these unbearable and unendurable pain. In approaching the study from psychological perspective, mainly two approaches have been identified as the method of study. The first approach is retrospective analysis, a psychological autopsy or psychological-autopsy in which clinicians and researchers piece together information from the subject's past (Jacobs and Klien, 1993). In which, relatives, friends, or therapists may remember past statements, conversations, and behaviour that shed light on a suicide. The second approach is retrospective information which may also be provided by the suicide notes that some victims leave behind. However, these sources of information may not always be available as less than one-quarter of all suicide victims have been in therapy (Fleer and Pasewark, 1982), and less than one-third leave notes prior to committing suicide (Black, 1993; Leenaars, 1992, 1989).

Sociological Perspective

Contrary to psychological approach, sociologists tend to overlook the internal makeup of the individual's psyche, rather the focus is emphasised on the external constrains and conditionings, a *social fact* in Durkheimian terminology. Since, suicide is a social fact to sociologists, primarily determined by both the social cohesiveness and structural constrains of the members of the group/society, there is variations in the suicidal rates depending on gender, age, rural-urban, race, religion, occupational status and marital status. Durkheim's theory considered the propensity of an individual to commit suicide is intrinsically related to two basic concepts: (1) levels of social integration, and (2) levels of social regulation. By 'social integration' Durkheim meant the way in which people come to see and feel themselves to be part of a society or a particular group. An integrated individual feels secure because he/she feels wanted/or needed by others. Without this sense of belonging, Durkheim (1979 [1897]) argued, people felt 'lost' and 'worthless', as it were from the normal activities of the society into which they were born. 'Social regulation' means 'the ways in which social groups/societies attempt to control their members' range of behaviour.' He believed that people who were integrated strongly into social groups, and whose desires and aspirations were regulated by social norms were less likely to commit suicide. Based on these two principles, he identified four types of suicide, in accordance with the relative presence or absence of integration and regulation. The first and foremost form of suicide is identified as *egoistic* form of suicide. Here, due to lack of or less social cohesiveness and integration among the members of society or social groups, individuals no longer feel their need or purpose to be in the society, at the same time individuals have no social support needed to handle the stress. The second form is known as *altruistic* suicide (over-integration) resulted from too much integration of the individual with group, where the individual lost its embodied independent identity from the group. For instance, in Indian context, the customary practice of *sati*—where the widows burn themselves in the funeral pyre of their dead husband is one such example. In the Japanese tradition, the practice of *seppuku* or *hara-kiri* by the warriors to avoid dishonour of themselves and their clan is also yet another example of altruistic form of suicide. *Anomic* suicide is the third form of suicide, and it is found in the social milieu where social regulations are weak and a state of 'normlessness' exist; such form of suicide occurred during the great depression in the 1930s. Related to which, Nisbet (1965) noted that *anomic* suicide is the consequence of sudden dislocation of normative systems where the norms and values by which individuals have lived for a lifetime breaks down. In this respect, *anomic* forms of suicide become a possibility when an individual becomes uncertain about the world in which he/she lives. The final form of suicide is *fatalistic* suicide emphasised on 'over regulation'. This form of suicide was observed by Durkheim to be the opposite of *anomic* suicide and was seen to occur amongst social groups that suffered from oppressive social discipline and regulation. Even, Halbwachs (1930) identified a concept of 'social isolation' where individuals who were socially isolated, in some way, suffered from a form of under regulation/lack of social integration and this made them more susceptible to suicidal forms of behaviour. Sainsbury (1956) found that there is a relationship between the highest recorded levels of suicide with highest levels of social isolation and social mobility.

However, the concept of social integration used by Durkheim is not clearly defined making it difficult to operationalized the concept, as argued by Gibbs and Martin (1964); therefore, alternatively, they proposed to use the concept of 'status integration' to measure the extent to which an individual's different social statuses overlapped. According to Gibbs and Martin (1964), the greater the level of social support he/she is able to get from his other statuses in life (father, employee and so forth), the less likely he/she is to actually commit suicide. Durkheim's inferential statistical analysis of suicide was criticised by Bilton (1996), arguing that that suicide is the product of meaningful categorisation by officials investigating agencies and it cannot be assumed that these officials share the same meanings on which they base their interpretations. Based on this premise, two main implications are evident, i.e. suicide rates and suicide statistics are not necessarily 'facts' as Durkheim had claimed. On the contrary, like all official statistics, the determination of suicide involves a social process of interpretation by numerous social actors. Therefore, Bilton (1996) argued that there is no real way of determining either the reliability or validity of suicide statistics.

To bridge the gap in the issue of reliability, according to Douglas (1967), we must understand the social act of suicide; we must understand how it is socially defined by significant social actors (the police, the medical practioners, investigators and so forth). We must attempt to understand the meanings that suicidal individuals "construct" for their actions. For Douglas, the person who intends to commit suicide can attempt to convey to others the meaning of their act (through the use of "suicide notes", the way in which they construct their death and so forth). The researcher, therefore, needs to get as close as possible to the world which he or she is attempting to study and the "most appropriate" methods of investigation involve such things as participant observation (of the people involved in the social construction process), in-depth interviews, personal documents, case studies of individual deaths.

According to Freud (1936) when death instinct dominates over life instinct then feeling of extreme depression and mood disorder emerges. Instinct and depression are not self-inbuilt but emerge due to negative changes in structural conditions where the individual lives. Durkheim emphasized on constructive process of suicide though he ignored the process. So, to comprehend the suicide among cultivators we have to understand the structural conditions of the society.

The predominant perspectives in the comprehension of suicides are psychological—social psychological and sociological. The conception and causes of suicides vary with these perspectives.

Review of literature on this problem indicates that most of the studies on suicide were conducted in Western countries that also in urban areas and very few studies were conducted in the developing countries.

After going through the literature on the recent trend of Indian studies, it can be observed that researchers have given much emphasis on suicide of farmers because recently in India the suicide of farmers has become a big problem for the society. So the major studies show that debt, crop failure, economic hardships are the leading causes of the suicides. Studies of the states like Andhra Pradesh, Karnataka, Maharashtra, and Punjab reveal that debt, crop failure, economic hardships are the leading causes of suicide among cultivators. Besides this, domestic discord, alcohol and drug abuse were also contributing to suicides (Shiva and Jafri, 1998; Deshpande, 2002; Assadi, 1998; Revathi, 1998; Vasavi, 1999). Surveys conducted in Punjab attributed suicides among cultivators to crop failure and high intensity of indebtedness among cultivators ['Movement Against State Repression' (MASR) 1998; Iyer and Manick, 2000; Kumar and Sharma, 1998; Association for Democratic Rights, 1998]. Mohanty (2005) tried to comprehend the phenomenon of suicides among cultivators in Maharashtra. He found that the rate of suicides among small landholders is more as they devote 60 per cent of their total land for cultivation of genetically modified cotton which requires both capital and labour intensive farming; therefore, crop failure present a challenge to livelihood. Even though different sizes of landholders are cultivating high yielding varieties of crops that require more capital, differential consequences are observed on the basis of landholdings. Most of the small sizes of landholders fail to recover the production cost and thus fail to repay the borrowed loan either from formal or informal agencies or both. However, larger sizes of landholders experienced more intensity of family quarrels, business failures, degradation of social status and power that seems to have contributed to suicides among rich peasants. Sharma and Mohan Kumar (2006) further support these findings on the basis of their study in Kerala. Jodhka (2006) observed that drought leads to differential consequences on the basis of size of landholdings. It affected more intensively the small cultivators and resulted in downward social mobility in terms of landholdings leading to loss of status in rural life. Narasimha and Suri (2006) found supportive evidence to the earlier studies from their study in Andhra Pradesh. Mishra (2006) compared the normal cultivators with the suicide victim cultivators and found that indebtedness in proportion to the asset what the suicide victims owned is very high than the normal cultivators. In addition to this, the suicide victims' households have larger size of family with more women and non-workers. Sridhar (2006) observed that the suicides are concomitantly related to the shift in cropping pattern from traditional rain fed cereal crops to commercial crops in the recent past in Andhra Pradesh. Satynarayan (2011) in his study "Suicide among cultivator in Sangroor" finds that shift of family values, individualism towards collectivism and luxurious life style of youth are the causes of suicide.

However, these above-mentioned studies have given a scant attention to the following issues: firstly, the integration of the individual with institutions like family, domestic discord, economic, alcohol and drug abuse are also the causes of suicide which, need to be comprehended more systematically. Secondly, the use of loans and its recovery process by formal and informal lending agencies also to be understood that affects the family and individual in terms of social isolation, feelings of degradation of status, disintegration of joint household and dropout of the children from schools. Thirdly, the occupational diversification of the family and the urban support system to the rural kin also needs to be looked in order to comprehend this phenomenon more holistically in a comparative framework. An interdisciplinary attempt is made to realize the impact of the indebtedness on status order, i.e. its effect on status, honour and prestige. If the status order goes down, then its relation with feelings of helplessness, hopelessness, isolation, worthless life, reduces social interaction and thus leads suicide. The recent suicide studies in India emphasise poverty, situational factor as well as social factor as a cause of Suicide. NCRB data shows that the low education, illness and family problems are the major cause of suicide. General perception about Sikkim is that there is no problem regarding, poverty and education. Although, employment was not a problem till recent times but today it has become one of the pressing problems in Sikkim. The State is pressed with the major problem of drug abuse/alcoholism. From our previous discussion in this chapter, we know that Suicide is another major issue which the State is facing since 2008 and urgent interventions are needed to tackle the problem.

On the basis of the above discussion, the following hypotheses were put forward to test:

Hypothesis

- H^0: Suicide is the resultant cause of the existing structural constraints and social inequality among various social groups (Ethnic, Caste, and Class) in the society.
- H^1: The gender disparities in the rate of suicide in Sikkim are primarily due to differences in their emotional and social attachment with the family/society.
- H^2: Alcoholism is one of the major factors contributing to suicide; alcoholism in Sikkim is the product of cultural practices and unrestricted accessibility.
- H^3: Financial constraints related to illness along with gap in accessibility of health facilities contribute to suicide.
- H^4: The changing family structure and familial ties in rural Sikkim is contributing to suicide.
- H^5: Acculturation stresses due to global cultural influences and imitation is triggering suicide among the youth in particular.
- H^6: Religious disparity in the rate of suicide is due to presence or lack of integrating element the practice of religion itself.

Based on the hypotheses, the study was designed to study the Psycho-socio processes of suicide and its unknown and known causes. It was also essential to study the role of cultural and social milieu

(Family, Education and Society) both in abating and escalating suicide rate and also the role of personal factors (needs, desire, personality, etc.) in escalating and abating suicide.

The study, was also designed to examine the role of demographic variable in guiding the behaviour of individual. For this purpose, the study was conducted in three phases. The first phase dealt with the statistical analysis of the last 10 years (2007-2016) data on suicide, the second phase dealt with the study of 242 suicide cases which had been sampled out from the data of 351 suicide cases provided by funding agency for the study, which was part of the data compiled from 2014-2016. In the third phase narratives of the victim were gathered through psychological autopsy. A total of 35 suicides had been studied for the purpose.

Phase I

As highlighted above, the first phase dealt with the statistical generalisation of the suicide cases of 10 years (2007-2016). The information had been collected from the Police Headquarters and Crime Bureau, Gangtok. The statistical analysis is primarily focused on charting the socio-demographic profile of the victims on the one hand, and on the other to determine or construct the prevailing pattern of suicide in Sikkim over the last 10 years.

Phase II

The second phase of the study was a partial extension of the first phase; here, we did in-depth statistical analysis of 242 samples (Z). These 242 samples were sampled out from the 351 (N) suicide cases provided by funding agency for the study. The data/information provided by the department was limited only to name, age, sex, and address. Excel stats and graph pad prism were used for tabulating the information.

The sample size was proportionately divided as per the database provided by the funding agency of individuals those who had committed suicide between, 2014 and 2016. During the field study conducted, out of proposed n = 250, only 242 samples were taken for research and analysis of statistics as the rest left out were repetitive samples.

Table 1.6: Final experimental tabulated research database of Z = 242 samples whose statistical analysis was done to infer conclusions

North	10 (4.13%)
East	69 (28.51%)
West	79 (32.64%)
South	84 (34.71%)
Total	Z=242 (100%)

The above Table 1.6 shows the study of 242 suicide cases which has been surveyed from the data out of 351 suicide cases provided for the study, which was part of the data compiled from 2014-2016 data.

Phase III

The third phase was undertaken to identify the role of socio-psychological factor as mediator in suicidal behaviour. The 35 cases were sampled using snowball and purposive sampling method. For this, Psycho-autopsy was used as a method and interviews were also conducted with close member (family/friends) of the suicide victim. In the psycho-autopsy, we interviewed the family members, close kins, and any other people who have lived with the suicide victims for at least last 15 days prior to the death of the victim.

Narrative analysis is a relevant tool as it is about documenting the serial of events sequentially that led to the final act of suicide by the victims. This helped us to decode the various factors that had contributed to the act by the process of psycho-autopsy of the family members, dear kins and friends of the victim. Here, it is important to mention that the methodology popularised by Clifford Geertz known as 'thick description' was helpful in the further analysis of the narratives, as the idea of 'thick description' entails about not just analysing of the narration about the behavioural activities of the victims but also contextualising those narrations in relation to the social setting which made the individual behave so, so that it becomes meaningful to the researcher. Linking from the psychology viewpoint, Bruner (1990) calls it "narrative mode of knowing" which gives privilege to the lived experiences rather than logical positivist constructs about variables and classes. Narratives provide insight into people's thoughts, feelings, and words as they deal with issues of loss, sometimes failing and sometimes succeeding. Stories can heal as they endow experience with meaning. Harvey (1996) poignantly states, "Without the pain that comes with significant loss, there can be no story. Without the story telling, there can be no meaning. Without meaning, there can be no healing." Since suicide and their psycho-social process had to be understood retrospectively within the participants, narratives were considered an apt tool of inquiry, giving ample space to participants for reflecting back and forth in making sense of their experiences with the deceased.

Interview Setting

Thirty-five narratives were taken for the study, consent was taken from the participants, rapport formation and informal interactions with the participant was done so as to develop a sense of familiarity and also apprise them about the study. Confidentiality of participants was maintained and each of the deceased was also given a code.

The inquiry centred on eliciting information on the family background, Socio-economic status of the victim, any behavioural changes, phrases and words which the victim would have mentioned or used.

Data Analysis and Theoretical Sampling

The first round of narratives was transcribed in order to code and to filter out the emerging codes and categories. Grounded theory involving three levels of coding, first level coding focused on line-by-line coding for obtaining the narrative data and helps to label vivo codes. Second level coding began, which is an aggregation of first level codes into categories. This helped the researchers to develop a codebook that included a list of emerging categories, preliminary descriptions of these categories, inclusion and exclusion criteria of these categories, and exemplars of text. Third level coding, also called theoretical coding, denoted a theoretical or hypothesis driven thought processing in analyzing and coding the data. Several techniques were used to facilitate the analysis. Theoretical sampling which included several second interviews with the selected participants.

In the following chapter, there will be discussion on the socio-economic scenario and emerging challenges which the tiny Himalayan state is experiencing.

Notes

1. "Mental health bill decriminalising suicide passed by Parliament". *The Indian Express*. 2017-03-27. Accessed on 2017-07-27 from http://indianexpress.com/article/india/mental-health-bill-decriminalising-suicide-passed-by-parliament/
2. As recent as there was a suspected case of Sati in Latur district in Marathwada region of Maharashtra was reported in *the Indian Express* daily newspaper dated April 1st, 2015. The news article can be accessed from http://indianexpress.com/article/india/india-others/suspected-case-of-sati-in-lathur-womans-body-found-from-husbands-funeral-pyre/

2

Sikkim: Socio-Economic Scenario and Emerging Challenges

Introduction

Sikkim, located in north-eastern India, was an independent Himalayan kingdom, till its merger as the 22nd state of Indian Union on 16th May, 1975. The state is connected to the rest of India through Siliguri Corridor bordering Bangladesh. The state, shares three international borders, with Tibet (China) in the north and north-east, Bhutan in the east and Nepal in its west. Comprising a total geographical area of 7,299 sq. km., it is the second smallest state of India after Goa. Sikkim falls under the inner mountain ranges of Himalayas with elevation varying from 300 to 8,540 metres of which the habitable zone is up to 2,100 metre altitude which constitute 20 per cent of the total area of the state.[1] Sikkim is also partially home to third highest mountain peak in the world—Kanchenjunga (8,598 m), which is also revered as a guardian deity by the Lepchas. The state has 10 mountain peaks that rise above 7,000 metres, 84 glaciers and 315 glacial lakes. However, being rocky and precipitous slopes make agriculture, transportation, and communication difficult.[2]

The tiny state is known to the world as a mystique Himalayan picturesque representing peace and tranquillity, and to the rest of India as its first 'Organic' state. Sikkim is the realisation of the ideal Buddhist philosophy in practice and is also considered by many (both religiously as well as by its people) as 'the Blessed Land'. Sikkim is also known synonymously for its cardamom and orchids. This land locked state of India has many deep unfathomed beliefs, traditional knowledge and many virgin areas where it has numerous pristine landscapes covered with psychedelic orchids Dendrobium and Cymbidium (Das *et al.*, 2012). The aromatic and variegated valley when a blossom with *Gurans* creates mystiqueness of divine aura and makes belief the existence of Mother Earth—the Nature. Geographically located between 27°04′46″ and 28°07′48″ North latitude and 88°00′58″ and 88°55′25″ East longitude on the Eastern Himalayas, Sikkim is renowned for its tourism potential, Bio-organic farming and agricultural practices and for its important cross border strategic importance. The state has been divided into four districts, namely East, West, North and South, with its district capital at Gangtok, Gyalshing/Geyzing, Mangan, and Namchi respectively.

Demographic Composition

As per the 2011 Census report, the population of the state is 6,10,577. With a sex ratio of 899 per thousand men, 47 per cent of total population are the female population. District-wise East Sikkim happens to be the most populous district (46.45%). South district ranks second with 24.05 per cent followed by the West district with 22.35 per cent. North district with a population percentage of 7.16 is the least one and has distinctive socio-cultural and political features. Being isolated and out of reach for most part of the year during the earlier period, the Lachen and Lachung in North Sikkim has developed a distinctive administrative feature known as the Dzumsa system devised for local administrative purpose and has still retained the system. In terms of female population, West district has the highest percentage of 48.52 per cent which is higher than State average of 47.09 per cent, while the North district has lowest with 43.42 per cent of female population (Table 2.1).

The age composition of the population as per 2011 Census shows 10.5 per cent percentage of total population in 0-6 age group population. The population in between 19-60 age group which basically comprises the working population accounts to 57.8 per cent, out of which 54 per cent are males, while 46 per cent are females. The highest 45.38 per cent belongs to 19-44 age category, where 54 per cent are males and 46 per cent are females population (*Statistical Journal*, 2013, DESME).

Ethnic Composition: A Brief Historical Backdrop

The political history of Sikkim is said to have begun with the establishment of the Namgyal dynasty in 1642. The political processes

Table 2.1: District-wise population of Sikkim (2011 Census)

State/Districts	Male Population		Female Population		Total	
	No.	%	No.	%	No.	%
East	151432 (46.87%)	53.40	132151 (45.96%)	46.60	283583 (46.45%)	100
West	70238 (21.74%)	51.48	66197 (23.02%)	48.52	136435 (22.35%)	100
North	24730 (7.65%)	56.58	18979 (6.60%)	43.42	43709 (7.16%)	100
South	76670 (23.73%)	52.21	70180 (24.41%)	47.79	146850 (24.05%)	100
Sikkim	323070 (100%)	52.91	287507 (100%)	47.09	610577	100

Source: Statistical Journal, 2013, DESME.

of Sikkim, prior to its merger with India and establishment of democratic form of governance was primarily feudal, monarchical and theological in its nature. The establishment of democratic form of government after its merger with India has brought many socio-cultural and economic changes along with the political transformation.

Like many other states of India, Sikkim is a multi-ethnic, and multi-lingual state and is a mixed bowl of culture where many ethnic communities and tribes have evolved their cultural identity. Ethnically, the state is inhabited predominantly by three ethnic groups, namely the Bhutia, the Lepchas and the Nepalis. Lepchas are considered as the autochthonous tribes of Sikkim, followed closely by the Bhutias. The consecration of first Bhutia King Phuntso Namgyal in 1642, led to the establishment of the Namgyal dynasty. The two communities enjoy the privileges as the original inhabitants of Sikkim (Singh, 1993: xii). Originally, the land of Lepchas, Sikkimese society bears strong influence of Tibetan Lamaist tradition and strong Hinduism as well. The benevolent early Lepcha rulers and later Buddhist influence has shaped social and political evolution of the state (HDR, 2015: 4).

The term Nepali is a generic term and is not a single homogenous entity, having culturally, linguistically and socially diverse communities. It incorporates many tribes of ancient *Kiratas*, like Limboos, Khombu-Rais and Yakhas; ancient tribes of Khasas, like Bhahuns, Chettris, Kamis, Damais, Sarkis, Newars. There are also the analogous ethnic tribes of *Kiratas*, like Sunwars, Magars, Gurungs, Bhujels, Thamis and analogous ethnic tribes of Khasas like Thakuris,

Jogi/Sanyasis, Majhis etc. (Subba, 2009). State Socio-economic Census, 2006 identified 21 communities in Sikkim including the others who are mostly the plainsman communities like Biharis, Marwaris etc. who are mostly engaged in trade, commerce and business. Religiously, the population is predominantly Hindu (57.76%), followed by Buddhist with 27.39 per cent of the total population, Christianity (9.91%), Islam (1.62%), Sikhs (0.31%), Jains (0.05%) and 2.67 per cent are other religions (Census of India, 2011). Bhutias and Lepchas are predominantly Buddhist, while the Nepalis are predominantly Hindus. The animistic and shamanistic traits are found in their practices of many of their communities.

Social Categories

All communities of Sikkim are divided into five Social categories. Scheduled Tribes (ST) category includes communities like Bhutia, Lepcha, Tamang and Limboo, Other Backward Class (OBC), Central list includes communities like Bhujel, Dewan, Gurung, Jogi, Kirat Rai, Manger, Sunuwar, Thami etc. while Other Backward Class (OBC), State List includes communities like Bahun, Chettri and Newar. Communities like Kami, Damai and Sarki are included in Scheduled Castes (SC) category while 'others' are mostly the plainsman communities, who have been residing in the state.

The ST population in the state accounts to 33.80 per cent as per 2011 Census whereas SC comprises 4.63 per cent of total population of the state. The State Socio-economic Census (SSEC) 2006, recorded the 'Others' category having the population of 9.2 per cent of total population. 74.85 per cent of total population resides in rural areas while the urban population comprises 25.15 per cent of the total population (Table 2.2).

Historically, Bhutia-Lepcha as a composite ethnic group (Nakane, 1966: 221) were regarded as the original inhabitants of Sikkim and Sikkim was considered as a Bhutia-Lepcha homeland. By virtue of being the original inhabitants of Sikkim they were identified as the 'Sikkimese'. However, the promulgation of Subject Regulation Act of 1961 by the then the Chogyal of Sikkim has conferred the Nepalis who were residing in Sikkim 15 years before the commencement of the regulation to be the Sikkim subjects, the status of Sikkim Subjects equating them as par with other two communities of Sikkim. Following the 8th May Agreement, 1973, the Government of Sikkim

Table 2.2: Scheduled Caste and Scheduled Tribe population by Residence, 2011

Social Groups	*Population*	*Particulars*	*Population & Percentage to Total Population*					
			Total		*Rural*		*Urban*	
			No	*%*	*No*	*%*	*No*	*%*
SC	28275 4.63%	Male	14454 (100%)	51.12	10496 (72.62%)	51.62	3958 (27.38%)	49.85
		Female	13821 (100%)	48.88	9839 (71.19%)	48.38	3982 (28.81%)	50.15
		Total	28275 (100%)	100.00	20335 (71.92%)	100.00	7940 (28.08%)	100.00
ST	206360 33.80%	Male	105261 (100%)	51.01	86059 (81.76%)	51.49	19202 (18.24%)	48.97
		Female	101099 (100%)	48.99	81087 (80.21%)	48.51	20012 (19.79%)	51.03
		Total	206360 (100%)	100.00	167146 (81%)	100.00	39214 (19%)	100.00
State	610577 100.00%	Male	323070 (100%)	52.91	242797 (75.15%)	53.13	80273 (24.85%)	52.27
		Female	287507 (100%)	47.09	214202 (74.50%)	46.87	73305 (25.50%)	47.73
		Total	610577 (100%)	100.00	456999 (74.85%)	100.00	153578 (25.15%)	100.00

Source: Statistical Journal, 2013, DESM&E.

Act, 1974, in its section 3 of this Act, identified the different sections of Sikkim population as (a) Sikkimese of Bhutia or Lepcha origin, (b) Sikkimese of Nepali origin, (c) Other Sikkimese, including Tsong and Scneduled Castes, for the seat reservations in 32 constituencies. This was further crystallised by the Representation of Sikkim Subject Act, 1974. Now based on the Sikkim subject status and said Act, Certificate of Identification (COI) is issued from time to time that differentiate local and non-local population in Sikkim. Sikkim Subject and COI is the basis of entitlement for various socio-economic and political resources in the state for Sikkimese of Bhutia, Lepcha and Nepali origin (Thapa, 2012: 11).

Presently, the organisation of the political institution of Sikkim followed the three-tier system of governance after its merger with India, and participated the general election for the first time in 1977.[3] There are one parliamentary seat (Lok Sabha constituency seat), and one Rajya Sabha seat in Sikkim. At the state level, 32 constituencies constitute the Legislative Assembly. Based on the reservation formula provided by the Representation of the People (Amendment), Ordinance 1979[4], which subsequently became an Act, 12 seats are reserved for Bhutia-Lepcha (BL) one seat for 'Sangha' representing the monks of the state, two for Scheduled Castes. The rest seventeen seats were considered as 'general' (Thapa, 2002).

Post-Merger Era: Socio-Economic Transformation and Challenges

Sikkim's merger in 1975 and the political transformation have led to massive structural transformation in the state. There has been immense expansion of administrative and bureaucratic structure and the state has focused, on considerable investment for all-round development of the State under various policies and programmes of the Central and State governments. The developmental initiatives of the State are visible in socio-economic transformation, which is manifested in various development indicators. The State also could not remain isolated from the Post 90s phase of Liberation, Privatisation and Globalisation. Therefore, along with the improvement in development pointers, development related social issues and concerns are also manifested in various forms. The following section highlights some developmental parameters which are followed by a brief discussion on emerging social issues.

Development Parameters

One example of the state's development initiatives is indicated by the state's prioritization of the social sectors. The government emphasized investments particularly in health and education and in between 2012-13, the Government of Sikkim allocated 37 per cent of its total expenditure to the social sector—from 27 per cent in 2001, which resulted nearly a sevenfold increase in nominal per capita social sector spending—from Rs. 4,810 in 2001 to Rs. 28,661 by 2012. Between 2001 and 2013, there were, on average, an annual increase in budget allocations by 12 per cent and 18 per cent respectively for education and health (HDR, 2014). The focus of State in educational sector can be seen from the improvement in literacy scenario.

Literacy Scenario of State

The literacy scenario of the state has improved considerably over the last few decades. The literacy rate of Sikkim in 1981, i.e. six years after merger with India was only 34 per cent which constituted 44 per cent male and 22 per cent female. The rate had increased manifold to 82 per cent in 2011—with 87 per cent of men and 76 per cent of women, who could read and write (Table 2.3). This indicates a laudable performance of the state in terms of educational sector, District-wise, the most developed East district came on top with 85 per cent, followed by South district (82%), West district (79%) and North district (77%) as per 2011 Census. The gender gap in literacy rates has come down to almost 11 per cent in 2011 from 16 per cent in 2001.

Table 2.3: Literacy Profile

Area	*1981*			*1991*			*2001*			*2011*		
	Male	Female	Total	Male	Female	Total	Male	Female	Total	Male	Female	Total
Rural	40.25	18.24	30.05	51.94	35.40	44.14	75.11	59.05	67.67	85.42	73.42	79.82
Urban	61.44	45.42	54.86	74.69	63.40	69.85	88.61	80.19	84.82	92.94	85.19	89.26
Sikkim	43.95	22.20	34.05	56.94	46.76	56.94	76.73	61.46	69.68	87.29	76.43	82.20

Source: Sikkim: A Statistical Profile, 2004-05, Directorate of Economics, Statistics, Monitoring & Evaluation, Government of Sikkim. Census of India, 2011.

State has also made considerable progress in terms of educational infrastructure. As per HDR, 2014, Sikkim has a strong network of 781 government schools, 421 private schools, 71 monastic schools, 25 local body schools, 11 Sanskrit schools and three Islamic schools. The state is also experimenting with alternative and innovative models of education. Sikkim became the second state in India to sign a Memorandum of Understanding (MoU) with the Quality Council of India on 27 March, 2011 for developing accreditation standards towards quality government schools.

The performance of the educational sector is also reflected in improvement in enrolment. Enrolment in primary and upper primary schooling is near universal, with net enrolment ratios being the highest in India. The gender parity index for enrolment in primary classes (I to V) in Sikkim is 0.98 compared to the all-India figure of 0.94. The net enrolment rate (NER) in primary education in Sikkim is encouraging. In 2007-08, 90 per cent children aged 6-10 years were enrolled in Class I-V. Only 10 States and Union Territories are ahead of Sikkim in this category. More girls have been enrolled in primary classes as compared to boys from 2005 onwards. The same trend can be seen in the middle and secondary levels as well. In 2005-06, the ratio of girls to boys suddenly dropped in favour of the latter in Classes XI and XII only. From 2007 onwards, this slight reversal has changed, with more girls enrolled at every level of school education in comparison to their male counterparts (HDR, 2014). Sikkim is ranked fourth among all states of India on the Composite Educational Development Index for 2012-13—a significant jump from the 12th position in 2011-12. Acceleration towards universal elementary education has reduced drop-out rates and increased retention at the primary level of education (*ibid.*). Sikkim's average drop-out rate at the primary level has come down from 7 per cent in 2009-10 to 2 per cent in 2011-12 (HDR 2015: xxv).

Health Indicator

Health is an important component of human development. There has been several benefits and substantial improvements in health sector that have ensued as a result of deliberate state interventions in Sikkim. The improvement in health infrastructure definitely is a positive indication in this direction.

The State has established a well-functioning primary health care system through a network of two Community Health Centres, 24 Primary Healthcare Centres and 146 sub-centres (Table 2.4). Health care is provided, among others, by 273 doctors and nine AYUSH practitioners. Except for the Sikkim-Manipal Central Referral Hospital, which provides secondary and tertiary care, there are very few private medical institutions. The state has four district hospitals and 1,560 hospital beds in 2012 or 2.6 beds for 1,000 people (HDR, 2014).

Table 2.4: Health Infrastructure in Sikkim

Health Institutions	*East*	*West*	*North*	*South*	*Total*
State Referral Hospital/STNM Hospital	1	-	-	-	1
District Hospital. Tadong Hospital	1	1	1	1	4
Community Health Centre	1	-	-	1	2
Primary Health Centre	6	7	5	6	24
Primary Health Sub-Centre	48	41	18	39	146
District Tuberculosis Centre	-	-	-	1	1
Centre Referral	1	-	-	-	1
Total	**58**	**49**	**24**	**48**	**179**

Source: Statistical Journal, 2015, DESM&E.

In addition to this, the State Government has the provision of supporting the travel and medical treatment costs of around 1,500 persons every year who are referred out of the state for tertiary care. The Government of Sikkim is also constructing its own state-of-the-art tertiary care hospital, with over 575 beds which will be expanded to 1,000 beds later. The hospital compound also houses a nursing college, AYUSH hospital, cancer care and rehabilitation centre within the premises (*ibid.*).

The state has initiated a progressive programme of Chief Minister's Annual & Total Health Check-up for Healthy Sikkim (CATCH) which was started in Sikkim in 2010, whereby the State started conducting an annual health check-up of all its citizens. The medical teams visit villages, homes, schools, and on other common gathering places and record medical history, examined patients, and conducts common blood tests. Although in the infancy stage, the programme has made a significant beginning.

Sikkim thus has recorded an impressive acceleration in human development with special focus in health indicators over the past decade. The benefits accrued as a result of interventions by the State. Following indicators highlights that State is making an improvement in health sector:

1. Health care in Sikkim is provided almost entirely by the public sector. Sikkim ranks highest among the north-eastern states. In 2004-05, per capita public spending on health was the highest in Sikkim which reflects the high priority accorded by the State to the public provision of health. The Government of Sikkim spent Rs. 1,082 per person every year on health as against the national average of Rs. 242. A direct

consequence of this has been the relatively lower burden of private out-of-pocket expenditures—28 per cent—as against almost 8 per cent for the average Indian in 2004-05 (HDR, 2014).

2. In terms of per capita health expenditure, Sikkim ranks highest among the North-eastern states with Rs. 1507, which is also much higher than the all-India figure of Rs. 1201. Nationally, Sikkim ranks 4th next only to Kerala (Rs. 2950), Goa (Rs. 2298) and Himachal Pradesh (Rs. 1511) (Annual Report to the People of Health—Ministry of Health and Family Welfare, Government of India, September 2012).
3. Sikkim has witnessed significant changes in the attitude of society towards Institutional delivery. Institutional Deliveries have also significantly improved from 32 per cent (NFHS 2-1997-98) to 47.2 per cent (NFHS 3, 2005-06), to 94.7 per cent (NFHS, 4, 2015-16).
4. Infant Mortality Rate and Under-Five Mortality Rates have shown an improvement from respective figure of 34 and 40 (NFHS-3, 2005-06) which has come down to 29 and 32 (NFHS-4, 2015-16).
5. Full immunisation coverage for children aged 12-23 months in Sikkim has increased remarkably from 69.6 (NFHS, III, 2005-06) to 83.0 per cent (NFHS, 4, 2015-16).
6. According to a recent report by the Comptroller and Auditor General of India, based on 2010-11 data, Sikkim ranked third after Arunachal Pradesh and Nagaland as the state with the lowest incidence of malnutrition in the country.
7. In 2005-06, Sikkim reported the lowest proportion of under-weight children (20%). Only 3 per cent of children under three were severely under-weight—as against the national average of 19.5 per cent in 2005-06 (HDR, 2014).

Despite the positive health indicators, the doctor-patient ratio is lower when compared with the World Health Organisation (WHO) standard norm of 1:1000 doctor-patient ratio.[5] The Sikkimese scenario is relatively worse when compared with national scenario which has been reported that for every 1,674 people one doctor is available in India. In Sikkim as per HDR 2014-15, the State had as doctor-patient ratio of one doctor per 2,500 population which has been shown as improved to ratio of 1902, while the population/Nurse ratio is reported to be 2993 (*Sikkim Statistical Journal*, 2015). WHO report on health workforce in India claims that Sikkim has only 0.12 per cent concentration of health workers. The report stated that "states with the lowest percentage of doctors were in the north-east: Mizoram, Sikkim, Arunachal Pradesh and Nagaland" (Anand and Fan, 2016: 4). Therefore, despite the overall increase in health indicators, this is an area where State can further focus on.

Economy and Work Participation

Seventy five per cent of Sikkim's population lives in rural areas. Therefore, the economy of Sikkim is primarily agrarian based and is restricted to traditional farming methods on terraced slopes for rice, maize, millet, wheat, barley, oranges, tea, large cardamom, and orchids. The net cultivated land as per Agriculture Census 2010-11 is 84159.91 hectares. Sikkim is known for cash crops like cardamom and oranges. In the high mountainous up to the limit of human habitation, agriculture is undertaken side by side with cattle rearing and cottage industries. Besides. Sikkim is also known for its breweries and distilleries industries along with many other pharmaceutical industries.

Table 2.5: Working population of Sikkim, 2011 Census

Sl. No.	*Item*	*2011*
1.	Population	6,10,577
2.	Total Workers	3,08,158 (50.5%)
3.	Main Workers	2,30,397 (74.77%)
	(a) Cultivators	82,707 (35.90 %)
	(b) Agricultural labourers	11,582 (5.03%
	(c) Worker in household industry	2,888 (1.25%).
	(d) Other Workers	1,33,220 (57.82%)
4.	Marginal Workers	77,741 (25.23%)
5.	Non-Workers	3,02,439 (49.5%)
	% of Total Workers to Population	50
	% of main workers to population.	38

Source: Sikkim Human Development Report 2014.

Table 2.5 shows that a total working population 3,08,158 accounting to 50.5 per cent of total population while 49.5 per cent are non-workers. Out of total workers, 2,30,397, i.e. 74.77 per cent of them are main workers. Among main workers category, 35.90 per cent are cultivators. 5.03 per cent are agricultural labourers. 1.25 per cent are engaged in household industry. A significant 57.82 per cent constitute other workers category. Therefore, agriculture related occupation still constitutes the dominant occupational category in rural areas next only to other workers category as per 2011 Census.

Among the states located in the Eastern Himalayan range, Sikkim is blessed with abundant water resources and exploiting this resource, the State Government has set up the Sikkim Power Development Corporation (SDPC) to tap the state's hydropower potential, which is estimated to be around 8,000 MW. Once the hydroelectric power plants are completed it will provide the employment opportunities to the local skilled, semi-skilled and unskilled manpower as well as create local business and contract opportunities.[6]

Tourism forms another important economic sector of the State, as the State is endowed with rich natural resources and bio-diversity and the State is a host to a number of cultural heritage and festivals. Sikkim has become one of the desired tourist spot in India generating tremendous revenues and livelihood for the people. The number of Tourist arrival in Sikkim has shown an increasing trend from 1000 visitors in 1980 to 1,16,500 in 1997 and has reached a current level of 2,00,000 per year.[7] Apart from this, the State promotes rural livelihoods and employment by using and investing in abundant natural and environmental bio-diversity and resources of state, by promoting creative activities like ecotourism, organic farming, and a host of other potentially income generating activities. The State is country's first and only organic state.

The developments as economic growth thus have been reflected in Sikkim's impressive growth in incomes over the past decade, which has contributed to the increase in HDI. During 1993 and 2000, the annual average NSDP growth rate was 5.75 per cent, however, during the last decade, between 2001 and 2012 on average 17 per cent annual growth rate was recorded, which is highest in the country. The fuel for such growth in the state was propelled by growth in industrial and manufacturing units, and service sector economy, particularly the tourism sector. This was evident in the fourfold increase in the real per capita income from Rs. 15,953 in 2001-02 to Rs. 69,202 in 2011-12 (HDR, 2014: 2015). The HDR further reports that in 2012-13, Sikkim reported a per capita income (net state domestic product) of Rs. 1,42,625—the highest among the North-eastern States, higher than all States and Union Territories with the exception of Chandigarh and Delhi, and more than double the all-India average of Rs. 68,757. Between 2004-05 and 2011-12, Sikkim's real per capita income more than doubled—from Rs. 26,690 to Rs. 70,477. In 2011-12, Sikkim ranked among the top five states in terms of per capita income. The impressive growth in Sikkim's Gross State Domestic Product is also attributed to commissioning of power projects over the Eleventh Plan period, 2007-2012 (HDR, 2014,2015:8).

Chakrabarti (2009) has observed that the economy of Sikkim at macro level is growing at the rate of 7.8 per cent from the analysis of 2000-01 to 2006-07 data. Growth is prominent in both the secondary and tertiary sector due to direct involvement of the government (Construction and Government jobs). However, a major concern noticed is a fall in the primary sector and its contribution in state's GDP over the years (Tables 2.6 and 2.7). This is also substantiated by Chakrabarti (2010), that food grain production and other agricultural yield has been "decelerating since 2000" and if the situation continues then it "is bound to increase rural poverty, both from the nutritional point of view as well as in terms of declining employment opportunities in rural areas" (Chakrabarti, 2010: 25-26).

1996-97 the growth rate of trade, hotels and restaurants has started picking.

Table 2.6: Contribution of Different Sectors to Sikkim's GDP, 2004-2012

(In per cent)

	2004-05	*2005-06*	*2006-07*	*2007-08*	*2008-09*	*2009-10*	*2010-11*	*2011-12*
Agriculture	19	18	17	16	14	9	8	8
Industry	29	29	30	30	35	55	55	59
Services	52	53	53	54	51	36	37	33
Total	**100**	**104**	**100**	**100**	**100**	**100**	**100**	**100**

Sources: CMIE and Government of Sikkim (for 2011-12).
HDR 2014, p. 8.

In addition to this, following economic indicators are also highlighted in HDR, 2014 which are significant:

- By 2011, Sikkim reported amongst the lowest percentage of population below the poverty line—8 per cent—across Indian states. In 2004-05, close to 1,70,000 people lived below the poverty line. By 2011, this number had come down to 51,000—a 70 per cent reduction in the number of poor.

Table 2.7: Sectoral Real Growth Rate of Gross State Domestic Product in Sikkim

(In per cent)

	2007-08	*2008-09*	*2009-10*	*2010-11*	*2011-12*
Agriculture and allied sectors	3.9	4.3	4.2	2.8	4.5
Industry	9.9	34.8	172.7	7.4	7.2
Services	7.5	9.6	24.5	10.5	10.5
Overall	7.6	16.4	73.6	8.1	8.2

Sources: Central Statistics Office (CSO) GSDP (2004-05 series), HDR, 2014, p. 8.

- Close to 93 per cent of households have electricity and 100 per cent have a latrine facility within the premises.
- Inequalities in the distribution of income and consumption have improved between 2004 and 2010. Sikkim registered the lowest Gini coefficient of urban consumption (0.186) across all Indian states in 2009-10.
- The Multidimensional Poverty Index (MPI) identifies overlapping deprivations at the household level across the three dimensions of the HDI (living standards, health and education) and low MPI value shows improvements in health and nutrition. It shows the average number of poor people and deprivations with which poor households contend. The MPI for Indian states varies from a low of 0.051 in Kerala to a high of 0.479 in Bihar. Sikkim ranked eighth with an MPI value of 0.150. Sikkim features as the 'best' in terms of the lowest levels of deprivation attributable to health and nutrition.

Gender Development Indicators

The multi-ethnic state of Sikkim is essentially patriarchal and gender based inequality is structurally inherent in Sikkimese society also (Thapa, 2009). The sex ratio (number of females per 1,000 males) although has improved from 875 in 2001 to 889 in 2011, it is unfavourable and low as compared to national average. However, one positive trend noticed is the child sex ratio (0-6 years) as per 2011 Census, is higher at 944, which is also higher than the national average of 914. The State witnessed significant improvement in Gender Development Index (GDI). Sikkim was among the top five states that recorded the maximum acceleration in the Human Development Index (HDI), which went up from 0.582 in 1996 to 0.665 in 2006. As per Human Development Report, Sikkim, 2001, the State registered a sharp rise in Gender Development Index from 0.445 to 0.528 in between 1991 to 1998 (Thapa, 2009:116). Women in Sikkim have benefited from educational and livelihood opportunities and women centric inclusive policies provided by the State government. The benefits of growth and human development in Sikkim are more equitably distributed today than they were a decade ago. Following facts substantiates and set the milestone for gender equality to a large extent.

- The gap between male and female literacy rates in 2011 has come down to 10 per cent as compared to 16 per cent in 2001.
- There is 50 per cent reservation for women in Panchayat. However, as per information based on Panchayat Cell, Rural Management and Development Department, 2013 women constitute 51.88 per cent of total Panchayat members.
- State government's policy of 30 per cent reservation of jobs for Sikkimese women in posts and services to be filled by direct recruitment under the State government and public sector undertakings resulted in fair representation of women in public sector (Thapa, 2009).
- The State topped in 2016 nationwide survey on States with the best working conditions for women.
- Sikkim fares well on the gender parity index across all categories of schooling compared with both other states of the north-eastern region and the national average. With the exception of Classes I-V, the female enrolment rate exceeds that of boys at all levels of schooling (HDR 2014, 2015:56).
- In terms of health and nutrition, women in Sikkim, by and large, enjoy better conditions of health and nutrition than women in other North-eastern States. The female infant mortality rate, 27 per 1,000 live births in Sikkim, is lower than the national average of 44. Similarly, the proportion of women whose Body Mass Index (BMI) is below normal, 11.2 per cent in Sikkim; it is the lowest among North-eastern States and considerably lower than the national average of 35.6 per cent (HDR, 2014, 2015:57).

Issues and Emerging Concerns

Development as economic growth is not an isolated process but also concomitantly accompanied by socio-cultural and political transformation, awareness, consciousness and socio-cultural consequences. Despite the fact that the State started numerous development initiatives and people centric programmes like Skill development mission, Social security mission, Poverty free mission, Self-sufficiency mission etc. and achieved many laurels for women and youth empowerment, there is a possibility that the development initiatives may not find equal reflections in all walks of life and might have brought new mechanisms of deprivations and problems in the state. Concurrently, the global trend witnessed in post 90s phase of Liberalisation, Privatisation and Globalisation, has brought many structural changes in the socio-political and economic domain and Sikkim could not remain isolated to this process also.

Therefore, the inter-section of these structural domains moulded the modalities of development in the state. The role of media and information technology, diversification in the economic activities, shift from primary to secondary and tertiary sector, growth of tourism industry, the process of urbanisation and modernisation directly or indirectly contributed to the growth of individualism, change in lifestyles, higher aspiration, competitiveness and culture of consumerism. The socio-cultural transformation often witnessed the weakening of collectivity, social ties and integration which characterised the traditional society. The transition and sudden exposure of closed traditional society with a strong sense of collective consciousness to a modern individualistic open society often have many ramifications like change in family structure, trend of nuclearisation of family, expansion of educational opportunities accompanied by outmigration from rural to urban led to so many social-cultural consequences both positive and negative, often leading to empowerment, cultural assimilation etc., On the one hand at the same time alienation and isolation on the other. These trends were also the characteristics of Europe what Karl Polanyi used the term 'period of the great transformation' to describe the massive social change which took place between 1750-1920 (Morrison, 2006) during the Eighteenth century, due to wave of Industrialisation and French Revolution. The massive industrialisation and rise of capitalism, demographic transfer and agriculture, urbanisation affected the degree of social attachment and integration to a great extent, which to Durkhimenian perspective were factors contributing to many social problems and suicide as well.

Contextualising this trend in Sikkim, despite the economic growth and all-round development, the tiny Himalayan state has encountered many social challenges and emerging issues like drug addiction, alcoholism, suicide and domestic violence, which cannot be overlooked in Sikkim. Following section presents a bird's eyeview of these emerging issues of concern.

Alcoholism and Substance Abuse

The consumption of alcohol is traditionally acceptable in the Sikkimese society and the easy availability of liquor tends to promote the habit. In the age group of 15-49 years, around 45 per cent of men and 19 per cent of women in Sikkim consume alcohol (NFHS-3, 2005-06*)*. Drug abuse has also been on the rise and is today one of the biggest challenges facing by Sikkimese society. A study on the profile of substance abusers in the emergency services wing of a tertiary hospital in Sikkim shows that the predominant substance abuse-related emergency attendance was related to alcohol (77%). In a retrospective study of emergency treatment seeking in Sikkim between 2000 and 2005, substance use emergencies constituted 1.16 per cent of total psychiatric emergencies (HDR 2014, 2015: 85).

Alcohol and drug abuse are important public health concern for the State to tackle which can be gauged from the fact that there has been an increase in the number of rehabilitation centres in the State. Substance abuse can lead to, and is often related to social decline, break-up of marriage, loss of job, and family ties etc. which may result in social isolation, which is also a potent cause of suicide, another major issue in Sikkimese society (*ibid.*, 62). According to the State Socio-Economic Survey 2006, one or more members consumed alcohol in 37 per cent of households, smoked *bidis* in 23 per cent of the households, and smoked cigarettes in 38 per cent. In addition, a little over one per cent of households reported usage of drugs (*ibid.*).

Domestic Violence

The National Crime Records Bureau (NCRB) reports show that crime against women in Sikkim is relatively low, a mere 0.02 per cent of the total cases of the country in 2008, which is also the lowest among the North-eastern States (*ibid.*: 41). Data from the National Family Health Survey (NFHS)-3 reveal that in 2005-06, levels of domestic violence reported by women 15-49 years was lower in Sikkim than in most other North-eastern States, and significantly lower than the national average which is close to 19 per cent of women in the age group of 15-49 years as against the national average of almost 40 per cent (HDR, 2014, 2015). However, as per the NFHS (August 2009), 16 per cent women in Sikkim are victims of domestic violence. One in every six women in Sikkim has experienced spousal sexual violence. This information is substantiated from the record of Family Counselling Centre (FCC) run by a non-governmental organization, the Association of Social Health in India (ASHI) and the State Social Welfare Board (SSWB), the active organization working for women's rights in the State. A scrutiny of record of the five years from March 2007 to 2012, indicates a total of 493 cases registered in the FCC run by ASHI (Association for Social Health in India), and FCC, located at Police Headquarters. The registered cases related to domestic violence indicates the major causes like adultery, alcoholism, bigamy, desertion by husband, torture and harassment by husbands and in-laws, and alcohol-related maltreatment and extra-marital affair, marital maladjustment etc. (Thapa and Lhasungpa, 2013).

Other Issues

The consequences of early marriages are many. It often hinders the prospects of education and the general trend is that that early marriage almost always brings an end to the educational prospects of the girl child. Culturally, early marriage and the traditional *Bhagaune pratha* (marriage by elopement) was commonly practiced among many communities of Sikkim. Even today early marriage do exist which is related to other social consequences. The mean age of marriage for girls in Sikkim has been put as 21.5 years in 2007-08. However, the percentage of girls marrying below 18 years in 2007-08 accounts to 16 per cent in the State as against national average of 22.1 per cent (Family Welfare Statistics in India, Survey Findings, NFHS, DLHS and Facility Survey, 2009). Early marriage and early parenting brings many socio-psychological consequences on women (Thapa and Lhasungpa, 2013). Heavy workload coupled with early marriages, between 16-20 years; take their toll on women's health. This is reflected in the declining sex ratio in the age group of 29-60 in Sikkim (HDR 2001).

Declining Agriculture and Unemployment

More than half of the population is engaged in agricultural practices. But, its contribution to the State's GDP is gradually declining since 1999 (Statistical Profile of Sikkim 2007), which is one area of concern. There is also a shift in occupational pattern from primary sector to secondary and tertiary. Further, it has been observed that unemployment is one of the biggest problems in Sikkim which is more prevalent among youth (15-29 years). Therefore, there is a need to explore how these demographic factors are contributing to emerging social issues like suicide.

Suicide

Sikkim's suicide rate was 37.5 per 100,000 people in 2015. That is not just more than triple the Indian average of 10.6 but way above the global average of 11.4. Further, it has been observed that unemployment is one of the biggest problems in Sikkim which is more prevalent among youth (15-29 years) and overall suicide victims (36%) are from this group (Sikkim Development Report 2008).

Verma and Sachdeva (2013), found youth suicide seemed to be related to high expectations created by development in vulnerable populations characterized by low income and status, who lacked the necessary skills for adjusting to the incoming forces of modernization and acculturation. In another study, Verma and Sachdeva (2014) found that disturbance in personal factors and structural factors are the causes of suicide. Structural/Social/Cultural factors (employment status, modernization, life style, child rearing practices, disturbed relationship, societal values, and generational conflict) and personal factors (high aspiration, high expectation, substance abuse, pre-emotional maturity etc.).

To sum up, the emerging social issues like suicide in Sikkim cannot be judged in isolation and must be studied in relation to other issues which are largely rooted in social structure. Therefore, the present study attempts to explore interplay of socio-economic, cultural and political forces which contributes to triggering factors for suicide. An exhaustive, discussion of socio-economic variables based on quantitative and qualitative analysis of empirical evidence will follow in the next chapter.

Notes

1. http://sikkim.nic.in/sws/home_int.htm
2. HDR, 2014 Sikkim
3. https://en.wikipedia.org/wiki/Sikkim_(Lok_Sabha_constituency)
4. Sikkim Extraordinary Gazette, No. 75, Dated 7.9.1979
5. Reported in the *Hindustan Times* published on 1st September, 2016, titled 'Healthcare crisis: Short of 5 lakh doctors, India has just 1 for 1,674 people'.
6. Sikkim Human Development Report 2014, p. 12.
7. http://www.sikkimudhd.org/gtkcdp/Chapter-3.pdf

3
Socio-Demographic and Economic Determinants of Suicide

Introduction

Sociologically speaking, as pointed by Jalles and Andresen (2015), the most common form of explanations of suicidal behaviour at the societal level is that of social conditioning which is associated with Durkheimian examination of suicide. Durkheim separated or rescued the phenomena or 'social fact' (in his own words) of suicide from the clutches of psychological/psychiatric domain to that of sociological interpretation. Durkheimian sociological interpretation of suicide heavily relied on the statistical generalisation of suicide, from where he was able to establish successfully the inferential pattern of occurrence, related to demographic distribution of the suicidy in relation to their socio-cultural, economic, and religious and political orientation, from where to come to the general theorisation to social integration and regulation. The present chapter is focused on highlighting the socio-economic and demographic profile of suicide victims. The profiling, as stated above, is important to come to a statistical generalisation and bring inferential interpretation of the data, and to see any correlations among the various variables or factors and social cause of suicide in Sikkim. The use of statistically representable data, in the study of suicide, began with Durkheim in sociological literature. The use of quantifiable information will help in establishing the phenomena by organising the information into identifiable pattern occurrence, "that they express sufficient regularity to require and allow explanation" (Merton 1987 cited in Goldthorpe 2001: 10). Merton has emphasised on the necessity of regularity or pattern occurrence, as it is "necessary for sociologists to recognize that their explanatory concerns are in fact with regularities rather than singularities" (*ibid.*). The establishment of regularities links the importance of statistics in sociology. Goldthorpe, further writes, (*ibid.*):

> If sociologists' *explananda* consist of social regularities of one kind or another, then statistics is, if not the only, at all events the most reliable and versatile means of demonstrating that such regularities exist and of clarifying their nature; and especially so, it might be added, in the case of regularities that are not readily apparent to the 'lay members' of a society in the course of their everyday lives but are revealed only through the—perhaps rather sophisticated—analysis of data that have been collected extensively in time or space.

For the purpose of qualitative analysis of the study, out of the 351 cases, 6 are from the North district, 114 from the East district, and 109 from South district and the remaining 122 from the West district of Sikkim. 260 cases are identified Sikkimese while the remaining 91 cases are non-Sikkimese or not stated. In terms of ethnic groups, Rai ethnic group has higher number of suicide cases (17.09%) followed by Chettri (16.81%) and Limboo (10.26%), and lowest suicide cases among the Bhujel, Jogi, Majhi, Sarki and Sunuwar 0.28 per cent.

Among Dewan, Sanyasi/Giri and Thami ethnic groups there were no cases of suicide reported.

Out of 351 (N) suicide cases given only 242 (Z) samples were surveyed using random sampling of each district from the cases provided by the funding agency. The determined sample size of each district is 75 (East district), 78 (West district), 87 (South district), and 10 (North district) of Sikkim. In the case of North Sikkim, although only 6 cases of suicide were provided, the sample size was increased to 10 in order to counter-balance the sampling error (Table 3.1).

Field research data covered only 242 (Z) samples owing to complex nature of the study, inability to collect the exact determined sample size, as some families were not available during the study, and few had reservations about sharing the information. Therefore, the sample size with which we worked is, East district (69), South district (84), West district (79), and North district (10) (as presented

Table 3.1: Total number of suicide cases given by DESM&E

Community	North				East				South				West				Grand Total	Total SSC/COI	None SSC/COI	Percentage
	Male	Female	Total	SSC/COI	Male	Female	Total	SSC/COI	Male	Female	Total	SSC/COI	Male	Female	Total	SSC/COI				
Bhutia	0	0	0	0	5	1	6	4	6	2	8	8	9	5	14	14	28	26	2	7.97
Lepcha	2	1	3	3	3	2	5	5	3	3	6	6	10	4	14	11	28	25	3	7.98
Tamang	0	0	0	0	9	4	13	6	9	1	10	9	4	0	4	3	27	18	9	7.69
Limboo	0	2	2	1	5	0	5	4	5	4	9	6	14	6	20	17	36	28	8	10.26
Bahun	0	0	0	0	8	1	9	5	3	5	8	8	2	1	3	1	20	14	6	5.70
Chettri	0	0	0	0	15	4	19	14	19	3	22	17	11	7	18	18	59	49	10	16.81
Pradhan	0	0	0	0	4	3	7	3	1	3	4	4	1	1	2	0	13	7	6	3.70
Rai	0	0	0	0	9	8	17	10	12	8	20	16	19	4	23	21	60	47	13	17.09
Manger	0	0	0	0	2	1	3	0	3	1	4	3	0	0	0	0	7	3	4	1.99
Gurung	0	0	0	0	3	1	4	3	1	5	6	6	8	3	11	8	21	17	4	5.98
Sunuwar	0	0	0	0	0	0	0	0	1	0	1	1	0	0	0	0	1	1	0	0.28
Thami	0	0	0	0	0	0	0	0	0	0	0	0	0	0	0	0	0	0	0	0.00
Jogi	0	0	0	0	0	0	0	0	1	0	1	1	0	0	0	0	1	1	0	0.28
Dewan	0	0	0	0	0	0	0	0	0	0	0	0	0	0	0	0	0	0	0	0.00
Bhujel	0	0	0	0	0	0	0	0	0	0	0	0	1	0	1	1	1	1	0	0.28
Majhi	0	0	0	0	1	0	1	1	0	0	0	0	0	0	0	0	1	1	0	0.28
Sanyasi/Giri	0	0	0	0	0	0	0	0	0	0	0	0	0	0	0	0	0	0	0	0.00
Kami	1	0	1	0	6	3	9	5	4	2	6	5	5	3	8	6	24	16	8	6.84
Damai	0	0	0	0	7	1	8	3	1	0	1	1	2	1	3	2	12	6	6	3.42
Sarki	0	0	0	0	1	0	1	0	0	0	0	0	0	0	0	0	1	0	1	0.28
Others	0	0	0	0	5	2	7	0	1	2	3	0	1	0	1	0	11	0	11	3.13
Total	**3**	**3**	**6**	**4**	**83**	**31**	**114**	**63**	**70**	**39**	**109**	**91**	**87**	**35**	**122**	**102**	**351**	**260**	**91**	**100.00**

in Figure 3.1). As per the gender data representation, it was observed that 50 per cent both males and females had committed suicides; in East district males (69.56%) had higher suicide percentage (females = 21; males = 48). In West district, males (64.56%) had higher suicide percentage (females = 28; males = 51). In South district, males (65.47%) had higher suicide percentage (females = 29; males = 54). We have not carried out any proportionate random sampling regarding the sex differences.

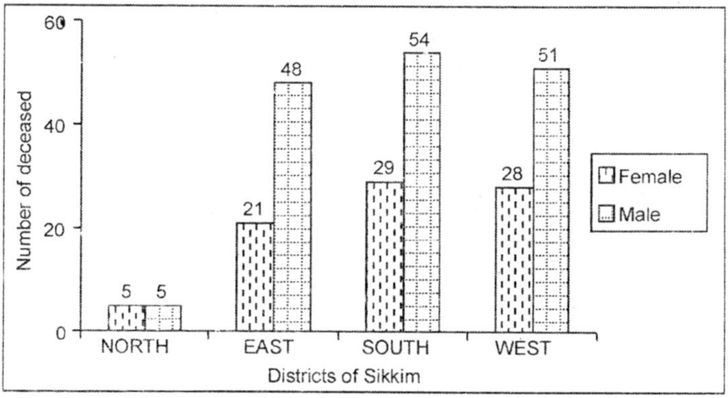

Fig. 3.1: Number of deceased's district-wise

Out of the 242 suicide cases which are being studied, 80.5 per cent (Figure 3.2; Figure 3.3) have EPIC number or who possess voter's identification card (ID), while the remaining 19.5 per cent does not have EPIC number. It can be said that either the victims were minors, for instance, as shown in Figure 3.4, those who belong to the age group of less the 15 years constitute 5.39 per cent. The second interpretation is based on the notion on the concept of Sikkimese origin and non-Sikkimese based on the possession of Sikkim Subject Certificate (SSC) or Certificate of Identification (CoI) or *Parcha* (land documents). From, the next Figure 3.3, it can be clearly observed that 34.44 per cent belongs to the latter category, while those who possess any of the above stated documents constitute 65.56 per cent.

Figure 3.4 shows the age range of the suicide victims, the highest is recorded among the age group of 16-25 accounting 30.71 per cent, followed by 26-35 age group (25.73%), and so on, the least is recorded among the age group of less than 15 accounting 5.39 per cent. The following Figure 3.5 shows the prevalence of suicide in accordance

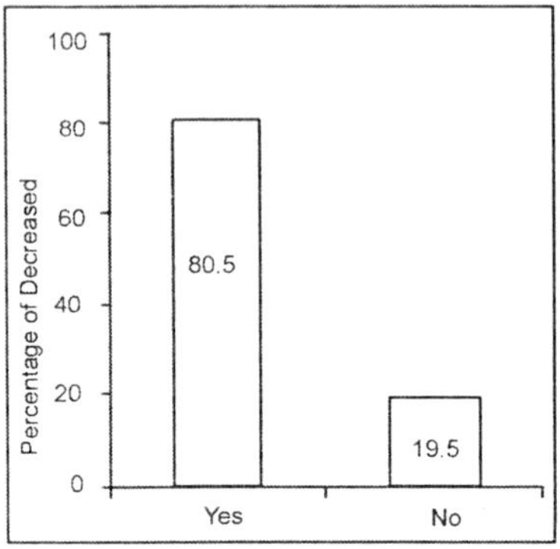

Fig. 3.2: EPIC or Voter's ID Holder

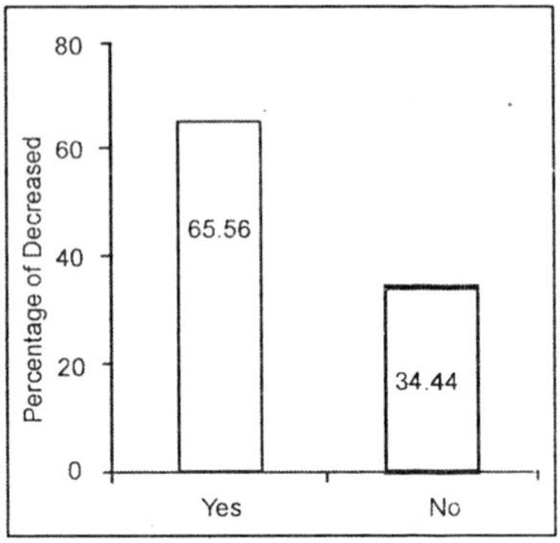

Fig. 3.3: SSC/COI/Parcha Holder

to settlement pattern. The graphic representation of the settlement pattern shows that suicide is more prevalent among the rural population (79.32%) as compared to urban population (20.68%).

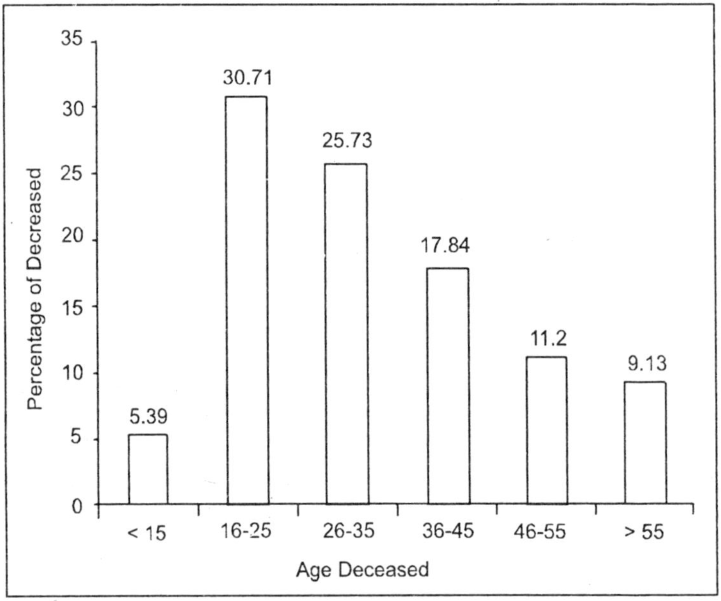

Fig. 3.4: Age Range of Deceased

In terms of the educational qualification of the suicide victims, it was found that 19.42 per cent were found to be those who have not

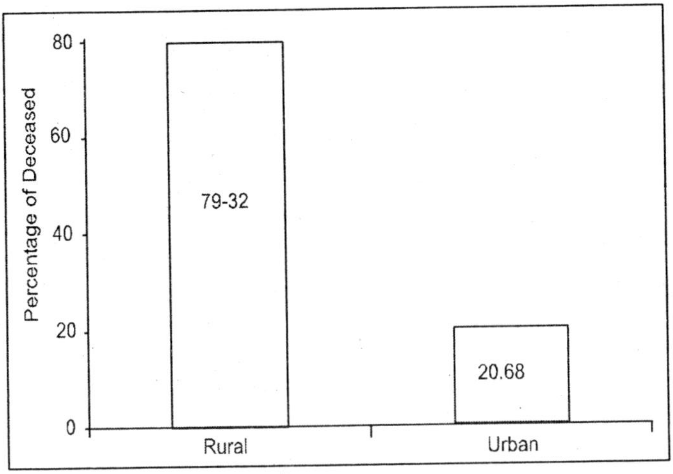

Fig. 3.5: Differentiation according to Residence

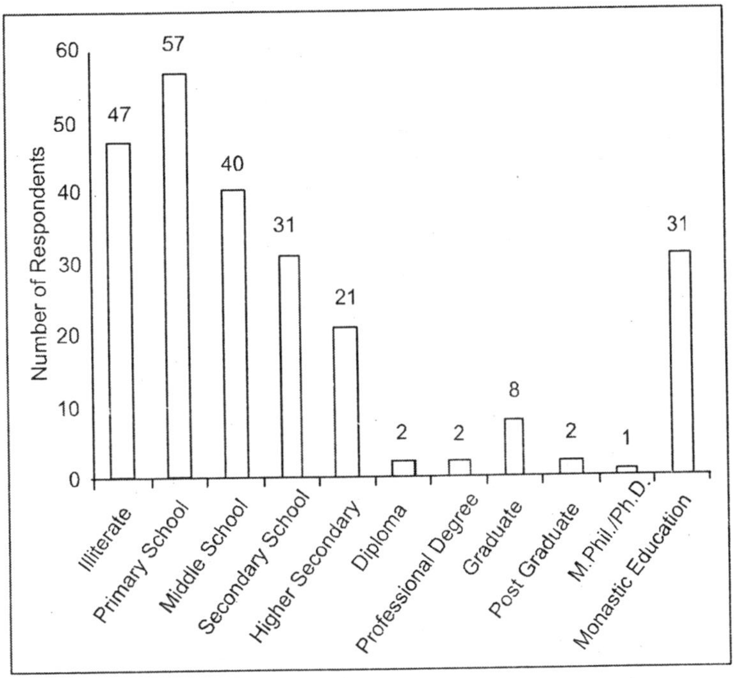

Fig. 3.6: Qualification of Deceased

entered into any kind of formal education, while the remaining 195 (80.85%) cases are from those who have entered any kind of educational system. Among this category, it was observed that the highest number of the suicide by those who have completed up to the primary education (29.23%) followed by middle school accounting 20.51 per cent of the total 195 cases followed by monastic education and secondary education accounting 15.9 per cent of the total cases Monastic education is common among the Buddhist communities like, Bhutia, Lepcha, Sherpa and Tamang. Although, traditionally it was customary/mandatory among Buddhist to send the one best son for the monastic education, now the general trend and observation is that monastic education is mostly opted either by the drop-outs or parents having low social, economic and cultural capital. This has also been argued by Lachungpa in her study about monastic education (Lachungpa, 2010), in an under-graduate study conducted for BA dissertation, it was found that monastic education is more prevalent among the lower socio-economic strata social groups.

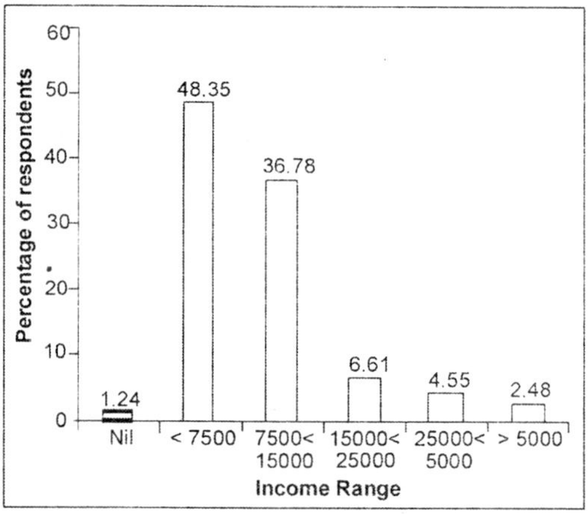

Fig. 3.7: Monthly Income of Deceased Family

The above figure shows that out of the total 242 cases of suicide, 117 (48.35%) of them belong to the income group of less than Rs. 7,500, per month followed by Rs. 7,500-Rs. 1,500 range accounting 36.78 per cent, while only three (1.24%) of them had no source of income at all. The data reflects that suicide is very much prevalent among those who have regular income as compared to no income group. However, the prevalence is more among the lower income group as reflected in the above figure.

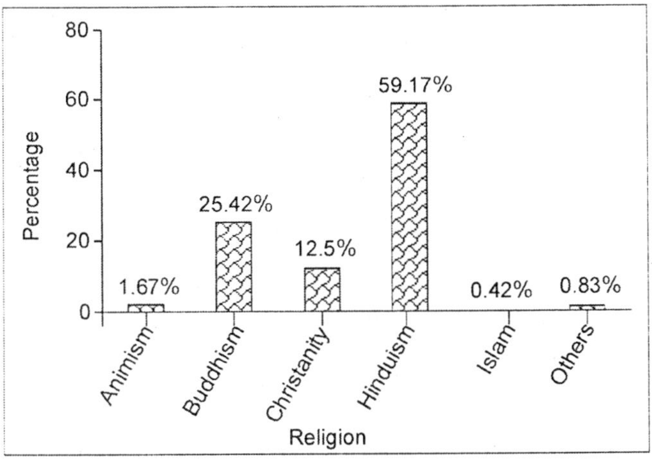

Fig. 3.8: Percentage of Deceased Religion

Religious distribution of the suicide victims shows that, as highlighted in the above Figure 3.8, there is a higher occurrence of suicide among the Hindus (59.17%) followed by Buddhist (25.42%), Christian (12.5%), Animist (1.67%), Others (0.83%), and Islam (0.42%). However, this alone cannot establish the occurrence of suicide by religion as the same proportion also applies to the population composition of Sikkim.

Community-wise distribution of the deceased showed that the incidence of suicide is more prevalent among the Rai community constituting 15.9 per cent of the total suicide percentage. Next to the Rai community, Chettri community has second highest suicide occurrence (13.81%), as shown in Figure 3.9, which is followed by Others (10.04%), Limboo (9.62%), Tamang (9.21%), Lepcha (8.37%), and so on. However, no case of suicide was found in the study among the four ethnic communities, namely Dewan, Jogi, Sunuwar/Mukhia, and Thami.

Although, the number of suicide cases in the study are shown high among the Rai, Chettri, and others; however, if we contrast the figure with the population ratio of each of the community then it reflects almost a proportionate case in all the communities of the state. However, it can be considered as high among the Damai, Kami, and Tamang, and lowest among the Bhutias.

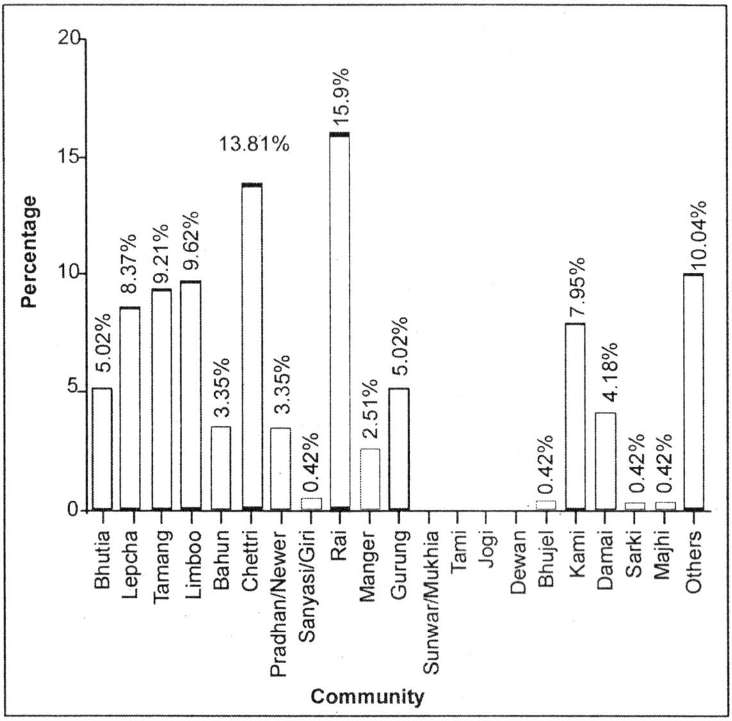

Fig. 3.9: Community-wise distribution of the deceased

Figure 3.10, represents the marital status of the deceased. Here, the result shows, that suicide is highest among the married individuals constituting 58.51 per cent of the total suicide cases in Sikkim. This is an important aspect of the study, as in most of the suicide cases, this aspect will be exploring further in the correlational analysis of various variables, particularly the marital status and cause of suicide.

The study found that, as shown in Figure 3.11, most of the suicide cases, i.e. 68.05 per cent, has one or more preceding suicide cases in the family prior to the suicide victim under study; while 31.95 per cent of the cases has first time occurrence in their family.

The study found that there is significant relation between suicide and alcohol consumption, as it is shown in Figure 3.12 that 53.53 per cent of the suicidy were habitual alcoholic, whereas, 46.47 per cent were non-alcoholic or social drinker. In relation to tobacco, the result shows that 4528 per cent of the deceased were tobacco users where the remaining were non-user.

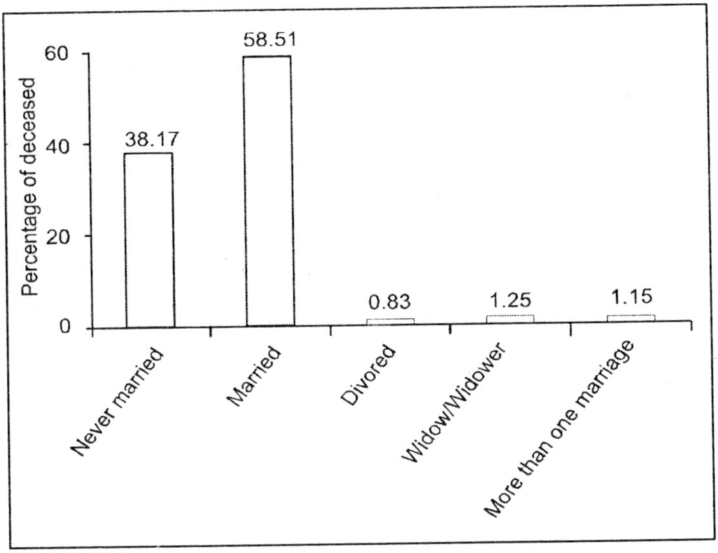

Fig. 3.10: Marital Status of Deceased

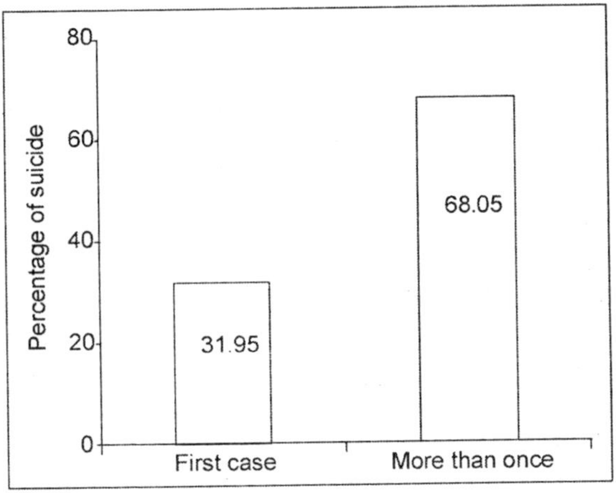

Fig. 3.11: Incidence of Suicide in Family

From Figure 3.13, it can be observed that, only 39.48 per cent belong to those individuals who have any kind of illness or sickness, leading to the act of suicide. However, contradictorily to the prevalent parlance related to suicide and illness, 60.52 per cent did not have any known major chronic illness before the act. Therefore, establishing

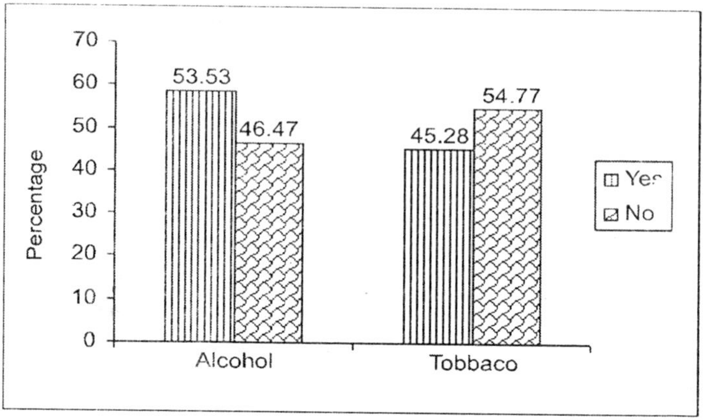

Fig. 3.12: Comparison of Alcohol and Tobacco Consumption by Deceased

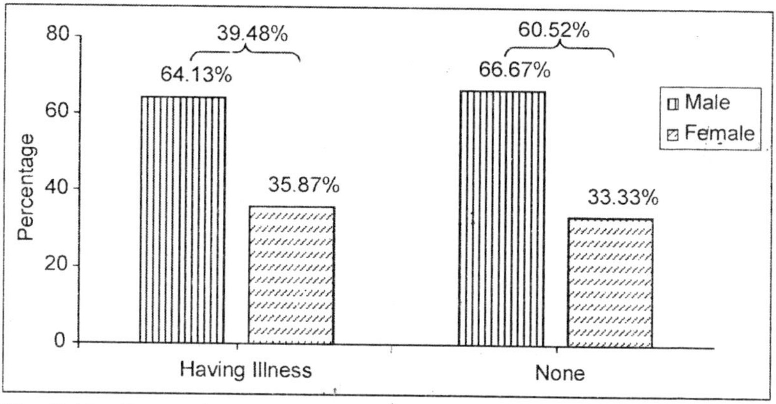

Fig. 3.13: Comparison between Suicidy having or not having Illness, and Sex Ratio

the correlationship between suicide and illness is not conducive at the same time generalisation is not viable. In relation to gender dimension, within the health scenario, men who are suffering from any kind of illness tend to commit more suicide than women, 64.13 per cent and 35.87 per cent respectively.

In establishing the various causes of suicide, it was found that people who have stress tend to commit suicide more. Stress is an adjusting process whereby a person adapts to changes. The adjustment as we will see later on is not only physical but also intellectual and psychological. The stimuli (changes) vary vastly and can be coming from the environment or even from the individual himself (WHO, 2016). However, stress cannot be the sole determining factor, as stress are in relation to other factors, such as relation problem, stress related to mental illness, financial problems, loneliness or idealness.

Figure 3.14 shows the predominant factor/cause of suicide, however, as pointed above, these factors overlap each other. The catalytic factors which work in junction with stress are discussed while analysing correlation as shown in Tables 3.7 and 3.8.

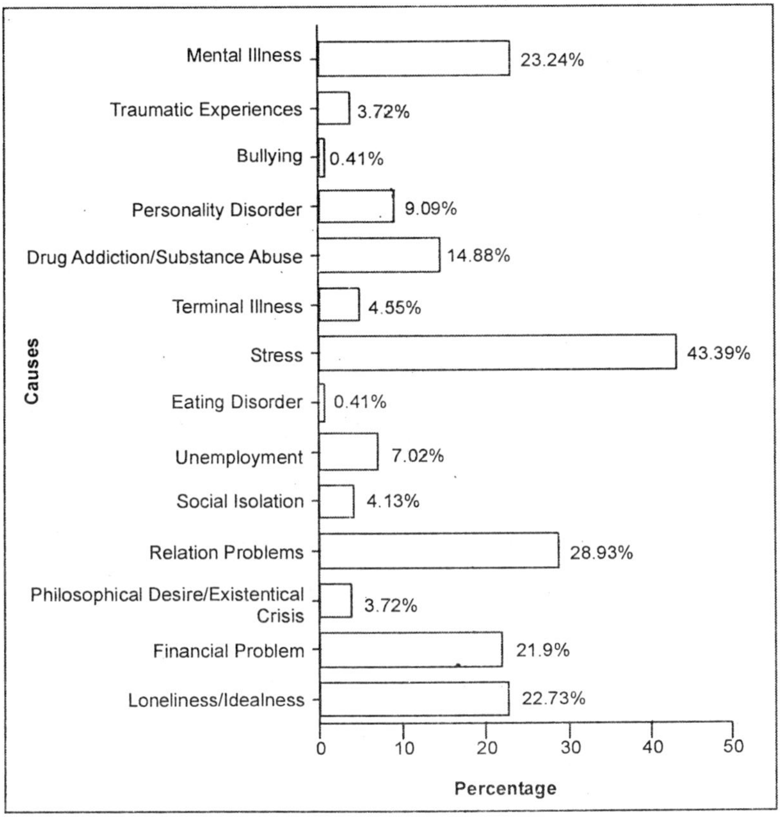

Fig. 3.14: Various Causes of Death

Table 3.2: Correlation analysis of dropout with types of occupation

	Dropout					
	Yes	*%age*	*No*	*%age*	R^2	*P-va*
Total	172	72.57	65	27.43	0.73	0.01
Occupation						
Student	10**	5.81*	32***	49.23		
Farmer	63	36.63	7	10.77		
Housewife	28	16.28	9	13.85		
Agricultural Wage Labourer	9	5.23	2	3.08		
Non-Agricultural Worker	3	1.74	3	4.62		
Salaried Government Employee	12	6.98	4	6.15		
Salaried Central Government Employee	0	0	1	1.54		
Salaried PSU	1	0.58	0	0		
Salaried Private Firms	6	3.49	1	1.54		
Business/Trader	4	2.33	1	1.54		
Muster-Roll	0	0	1	1.54		
Self Employed	8	4.65	1	1.54		
Contractors	1	0.58	1	1.54		
Unemployed	15	8.72	2	3.08		
Others	11	6.4	0	0		
Pensioner	0	0	0	0		

* Percentage of dropout with an occupation with respect to total number of suicidy who were dropout.

** Dropout respondents with an occupation (student).

*** Respondents saying "Yes" to an occupation (student) but "No" to dropout.

Table 3.2 shows the correlation of dropout and occupation with respect to suicide. Of the total sample studied, 172 suicidy were found to be dropouts constituting 72.57 per cent of the cases. The correlation analysis shows that there are higher cases of suicide among the dropouts who were engaging in the occupation of farming prior to their suicide (36.63%). This is followed by housewives (16.28%), unemployed (8.72%) and so on. However, if we see the significance of the correlation analysis, by measuring the gap between the percentage differences between those who are dropout and who are not, then, it can be established that there is higher occurrence of suicide among the farmers, next to it are unemployed, others, and self-employed. Therefore, there is a positive correlation between dropout and occupations such as farming, housewife, agricultural wage labourer, salaried private, business or trader, self-employed and unemployed which leads to suicide, as the percentage of population of dropouts bearing these occupations is higher than the population with an occupation without the issues of dropout. One way ANOVA was used and the results were statistically significant with p-value less than 0.05.

Table 3.3: Correlation with monthly family income and family size

Family Member Size		Total	NIL	<Rs 7500	Rs. 7500< Rs. 15000	Rs. 15000< Rs. 25000	Rs. 25000< Rs. 50000	>Rs. 50000	R^2	P-value
(1-3)	Yes	30	28**	19	5	1	3	0	0.857	<0.0001
	% age	12.39	6.67*	63.33	16.67	3.33	10	0		
	No	212	26***	113	54	11	4	4		
	% age	87.6	12.26	53.3	25.47	5.19	1.89	1.89		
(4-7)	Yes	182	21	96	50	9	2	4		
	% age	75.2	11.54	52.75	27.47	4.95	1.1	2.2		
	No	60	7	36	9	3	5	0		
	% age	24.7	11.67	60	15	5	8.33	0		
(8-11)	Yes	28	5	15	4	2	2	0		
	% age	11.57	17.86	53.57	14.29	7.14	7.14	0		
	No	214	23	117	55	10	5	4		
	% age	88.42	10.75	54.67	54.67	4.67	2.34	1.87		
(12-15)	Yes	2	0	2	0	0	0	0		
	% age	0.82	0	100	0	0	0	0		
	No	240	28	130	59	12	7	4		
	% age	99.17	11.67	54.17	24.58	5	2.92	1.67		

* Percentage of respondents belonging to a particular family size group (1-3) with a particular monthly salary (Nil) with respect to total number of respondents present in the particular family size group (1-3).

** Number of respondents belonging to a particular family size (1-3) with a particular monthly salary (Nil).

*** Respondents belonging to a particular family size group (1-3) but without having the particular salary (Nil).

The correlation of monthly family income with family size shows that suicide is high among the family size of (4-7) and (1-3) with lower income holders are most affected with respect to suicide prevalence. We can observe in Table 3.3 that the prevalence of suicide is very high in the range of 4 to 7 family members. Within this family size group the number of suicide committed are high among the monthly income range of Rs. < 7,500 (52.75%), followed by Rs. 7,500-Rs.15,000 (27.47%), and those who does not have regular monthly income (11.54%). However, statistically, the correlation between the family member size and income becomes more pronounced in the income group of Rs. 7,500-Rs. 15,000, as on the positive side it is 27.47 per cent and on the negative side it is 15 per cent, with a difference of around 13 per cent. One way ANOVA was used and the results were statistically significant with p-value < 0.05.

One way ANOVA was used and the results are statistically significant with p-value < 0.05. Table 3.4 shows the correlation of relationship problems with monthly salary, marital status, and age groups. The results confers that in case of monthly income there is an association of lower income holders in the range of those who earn less than Rs. 7,500 to Rs. 15,000 with relationship problems. For instance, as shown in the table, those whose monthly income is less than Rs. 7,500 have relationship issues contributing 42.03 per cent of those who committed suicide due to relationship problems (as also shown in Figure 3.14, which is the second highest cause of suicide in Sikkim). Second income range correlated with relationship problems causing suicide categorised under (Rs. 7,500 < Rs. 15,000), contributed to 10.14 per cent of the suicide cases. To sum up, in the correlation analysis, there is a positive relation between relationship problems and low income (those in the range of < Rs. 7,500 to Rs. 15,000); therefore, it may be conclude that lower income holders with relationship problems are more prone to suicide acts.

In case of marital status, the correlation analysis demonstrates that married population having relationship problems are more prone to suicide. As shown in Figure 3.10, a significant percentage of 38.17 per cent of suicide cases are among the never married individuals. However, the correlation analysis shows that there is a negative correlation between relationship problems and never married. So, we can safely generalised that the factor which cause never married to commit suicide is not related to relationship problems. Further, as shown in Figure 3.10, although the number of suicidy related to

Table 3.4: Correlation with relationship problems and monthly income, marital status, and age groups

Relationship Problems							
		Yes	*%age*	*No.*	*%age*	R^2	*P-value*
	Total	69	28.51	173	71.49	0.9	< 0.0001
Monthly Income	NIL	30**	43.48*	88***	50.87		
	< Rs. 7500	29	42.03	61	35.26		
	Rs. 7500 < Rs. 15000	7	10.14	10	5.78		
	Rs. 15000 < Rs. 25000	0	0	5	2.89		
	Rs. 25000 < Rs. 50000	1	1.45	5	2.89		
	>Rs. 50000	0	0	0	0		
Marital Status	Married	47	68.12	94	54.34	0.9	0.0006
	Never Married	19	27.54	73	42.2		
	Divorced	1	1.45	1	0.58		
	Widow/Widower	1	1.45	2	1.16		
	More than One Marriage	1	1.45	2	1.16		
Age Groups	<15	3	4.35	10	5.78	0.9	0.0007
	15-25	23	33.33	51	29.48		
	26-35	21	30.43	41	23.7		
	36-45	13	18.84	30	17.34		
	46-55	5	7.25	22	12.72		
	>55	4	5.8	18	10.4		

* Percentage of respondents having relationship problems with a particular monthly salary with respect to total number of respondents saying "Yes" to relationship problems.

** Respondents saying "Yes" to a particular monthly salary (Nil) and relationship problems.

*** Respondents saying "Yes" to a particular monthly salary (Nil) but "No" to relationship problems.

divorced, widow/widower, and more than one marriage is very less in number; nonetheless, there is a significant correlation with the relationship problems causing suicide.

In the matter concerning with age groups and relationship problems, those who are in the age groups from 15-45 are prone to suicide with the analysis variables. For instance, higher number of relationship problems related to suicide are more prevalent among the age group of 26-35, followed by 15-25, and 36-45, when the differences between the positive and negative correlations are compared.

Table 3.5: Correlation of Health Problems with Financial Problems and Monthly Income

		Health Problems					
		Yes	*%age*	*No*	*%age*	R^2	*P-value*
Total		99	40.9	143	59	0.9	<0.0001
Financial Problems	Yes	26**	26.26*	43	30.07		
NIL		44	44.44	74	51.75		
< Rs. 7500		42	42.42	48	33.57		
Rs. 7500 < Rs.15000		6	6.06	11	7.69		
Rs. 15000 < Rs.25000		3	3.03	2	1.4		
Rs. 25000 < Rs.50000		0	0	6	4.2		
> Rs. 50000		0	0	0	0		

* Percentage of respondents having both financial and health problems with respect to total number of respondents saying "Yes" to stress.

** Respondents saying "Yes" to both financial and health problems.

*** Respondents saying "Yes" to financial problems but "No" to health problems.

The correlation of health problems with financial problems and monthly income was carried out using one way ANOVA, and the results are statistically significant with p-value < 0.05. The results suggested that there is less impact of financial and health problem together on suicide as the percentage of population having financial problems but without health issues is higher than that population with having both financial and health problems, showing a negative correlation between the two. However, when it was elaborately analysed in relation to monthly income range, then we can observe that suicide is prevalent among those who have health problems with monthly income range less than Rs. 7,500 (42.42%), which was followed by (Rs. 15,000-Rs. 25,000) income range. Therefore, those who belong to lower income group (Rs. < 7,500) with health problems are prone to suicide (Ref. Chapter 4. Section on Health Problems).

Table 3.6: Correlation analysis of suicide between monthly income with alcohol, tobacco, and drug addiction

	Unemployment					
	Yes	*%age*	*No*	*%age*	R^2	*P-value*
Total	16	6.6	226	93.3	7.7	0.02
Alcohol (Yes)	10**	62.5*	119***	52.65		
Tobacco (Yes)	11	68.75	98	43.36		
Drug Addiction (Yes)	1	6.25	35	15.49		

* Percentage of respondents consuming alcohol + unemployed with respect to total number of respondents saying "Yes" to unemployment.

** Respondents saying "Yes" to both alcohol and unemployment.

*** Respondents saying "Yes" to Alcohol but "No" to Unemployment.

Table 3.6 shows the correlation of unemployment with alcohol, tobacco, and drug addiction. The correlation was established using Chi Square test and the results are statistically significant with the P-value < 0.05. The analysis shows that there is a positive correlation between unemployment and alcohol (62.5%), that is, unemployed population consuming alcohol are more prone to suicides than those of employed population consuming alcohol. Similarly, in the case with tobacco there is positive correlation with unemployment (68.75%); in fact, the correlation is higher than those with alcoholism. However, in case of drug addiction, the unemployed population were less affected than that of employed population involved in drug addiction resulting to suicide. This aspect can be further illustrated in relation to two reasons, firstly, higher number of drug addicts were employed individuals with some source of income which provided easy accessibility and dependency to drugs, which itself is a matter of concern. Secondly, during the field survey, it was found that most of the family members were not willing to share information related to drug addiction of the deceased as they feel that this could tarnish their *status* in society (Ref. Chapter 4, Section on Drug Abuse and Alcoholism).

Table 3.7 seeks to establish the correlation between stress with financial problems, relationship problems, unemployment, trauma, and previous suicide case in the family using Chi Square test. The test results are statistically significant with the P-value < 0.05. As highlighted in Figure 3.14, stress is the major cause of suicide in Sikkim, however, in the earlier analysis the causal relationship was

Table 3.7: Correlation between stress with other factors for suicide

	Stress					
	Yes	%age	No	%age	R^2	P-value
Total	102	42.3	139	57.6	12.92	0.01
Financial Problems	28**	27.45*	24***	17.27		
Relationship Problems	28	20.14	41	29.5		
Unemployment	11	10.78	5	3.6		
Trauma	6	5.88	3	2.16		
Previous Suicides in Family	68	66.67	34	24.46		

* Percentage of respondents with financial problems and stress with respect to total number of respondents saying "Yes" to stress.

** Respondents saying "Yes" to both financial problems and stress.

*** Respondents saying "Yes" to financial problems but "No" to stress.

not able to establish. The correlation analysis results shows that all the factors were positively correlated with stress resulting to suicide, except to relationship problems which shows a negative correlation. Among all the established correlation, individuals with earlier history of suicide in the family are more prone to stress resulting to suicide, as this factor accounts for 66.67 per cent in the positive correlation. Second to it, the most prevalent stress related to suicide is caused by financial problems, followed by unemployment (10.78%), and trauma (5.88%). The population having multiple problems were found to have considerable stress conditions with higher percentages than those population having no stress conditions.

The correlational analysis with stress and religion shows that there is negative correlation between religion with stress. As observed in the Table 3.8, that higher percentage of population in particular religions were without stress, except in the case of Christianity. Therefore, among the various religious denominations, Christians were found to be more prone to suicide in relation to stress related causes. Unlike other religions, Christians are likely to link closely with one another through their Sunday mass; therefore, sociologically explaining, this could primarily be due to resultant cause of negative social solidarity in relation to their social status, when people are more closely tied together in a community, the social stigmatisation in relation to failure in various aspects of life, alcoholism, previous suicide cases in the family, financial problems can work in reverse, as people always prefer a positive image in propagating or maintaining

Table 3.8: Correlation with stress and religion

Religion	*Stress*					
	Yes	*%age*	*No*	*%age*	R^2	*P-value*
Total	102	42.3	139	57.6	0.9	< 0.001
Animism	0	0	4***	2.88		
Buddhism	26**	25.49*	35	25.18		
Christianity	17	16.67	13	9.35		
Hinduism	57	55.88	85	61.15		
Islam	0	0	0	0		
Others	2	1.96	0	0		

* Percentage of respondents within a particular religion + stress with respect to total number of respondents saying "Yes" to stress.

** Respondents saying "Yes" to both religion and stress.

*** Respondents saying "Yes" to a particular religion but "No" to stress.

their social status. However, further exploration is desirable in this connection.

The correlation analysis of stress with religion is being studied using one way ANOVA and the results were statistically significant with P-value < 0.05.

Table 3.9: Correlation of alcohol, tobacco, and drugs with loneliness, social isolation and relationship problems

	Alcohol				*Tobacco*				*Drugs*				*P-value*
	Yes	%age	No	%age	Yes	%age	No	%age	Yes	%age	No	%age	< 0.0001
Total	129	53.5	112	46.4	109	45.23	132	54.77	36	14.88	206	85.12	
Loneliness	30**	23.26*	26***	23.21	21	19.27	35	26.52	4	11.11	52	25.24	
Social Isolation	6	4.65	4	3.57	3	2.75	7	5.3	2	5.56	8	3.88	
Relationship Problems	36	52.17	93	53.76	28	40.58	81	46.82	7	10.14	29	16.76	

* Percentage of respondents consuming alcohol with and loneliness with respect to total number of respondents saying "Yes" to alcohol.

** Respondents saying "Yes" to both loneliness and alcohol.

*** Respondents saying "Yes" to loneliness but "No" to alcohol.

Table 3.9 represents the correlation of alcohol, tobacco, and drugs with loneliness, social isolation and relationship problems. The analysis has been carried out using two-way ANOVA, the results are statistically significant with P-value <0.05. Analysis of the correlation

Table 3.10: Correlation analysis of suicide between monthly income with alcohol, tobacco, and drug addiction

	Monthly Income Range												R^2	P-VALUE
	NIL		<Rs. 7500		Rs.7500-Rs.15000		Rs. 15000-Rs. 25000		Rs. 25000-Rs. 50000		>Rs. 50000			
	Yes	No	Yes	No	Yes	No	Yes	No	Yes	No	Yes	No		
Total	118	125	90	152	17	225	5	237	6	236	0	242		
Alcohol (Yes)	46**	83***	60	69	11	118	4	125	4	125	0	129		
%age	38.98*	66.4	66.67	45.39	64.71	52.44	80	52.74	66.67	52.97	0	53.31		
Tobacco (Yes)	41	68	47	62	12	97	4	105	2	107	0	109	0.7	0.01
%age	34.75	54.4	52.22	40.79	70.59	43.11	80	44.3	33.33	45.34	0	45.04		
Drug addiction	15	21	15	21	2	34	1	35	1	35	0	36		
%age	12.71	16.8	16.67	13.82	11.76	15.11	20	14.77	16.67	14.83	0	14.88		

* Percentage of respondents with a particular income (Nil) consuming alcohol with respect to total number of respondents having a particular income (Nil).

* Respondents saying YES to both Alcohol + Nil (Income).

** Respondents saying YES to Alcohol but No to Nil (Income).

suggest that socially isolated population consuming alcohol is higher than that of socially isolated population not consuming alcohol, which is marginally shadowed by loneliness. Therefore, alcoholism and social isolation plays a significant role in the process of suicide. Likewise, in case of drug, similar analysis is generated from the data. So it can be assumed that, use of alcohol and drug in conjunction to social isolation has a positive correlation in suicide. However, in case of tobacco none of the considered variables had positive correlation.

Table 3.10 shows the correlation of monthly income with alcohol, tobacco and drug addiction. In case of alcohol consumption, the suicide is prevalent in case of lower income holders who consume alcohol. It can be inferred that alcoholism is one of the major cause of suicide, as also seen in Figure 3.12; however, the above correlational analysis between incomes with alcoholism shows that the association between the two is more prevalent among the low-income group. However, in case of Tobacco the middle-income holders (< Rs. 7500 = < Rs. 25000) are mostly affected with high suicide prevalence and similar is the case of Drug addiction, the middle-class population with income (< Rs. 7500 = < Rs. 25000) is prevalent to suicide. One way ANOVA was done and the results are statistically significant with P-value < 0.05.

4

Telling Stories

Narrative Approach in Qualitative Analysis

Introduction

Psychological autopsy as a methodological tool is used to gather the information in relation to the circumstances and context surrounding a person's death. The autopsy is performed as a narrative reconstruction and its consistency depends on the quality of information provided. Psychological autopsy (or psych-autopsy) is aimed at reconstructing individual's psychological makeup, i.e. lifestyle, thoughts, feelings, behaviours, intentions, motivations, psychodynamics and life circumstances, as well as the mode and details of the suicidal act (Hawton *et al.*, 2003). The psychological autopsy is usually based on personal interviews with acquaintances, review and analysis of records describing the deceased, analysis of suicide notes, and a comprehensive case formulation. Werlang and Botega (2003) elaborated and validated a semi-structured interview guide to study psychological autopsies in suicide cases, focusing on triggering factors and stressors, motivation, lethality. These included questions about social profiling, portrayal and way of life, description of the suicide, accompanying atmosphere and mental state of the individual. The tool presented by these authors, allows an objective and reliable understanding of the actual impact of stressful social-psycho events that motivated the suicide, through verbal and behavioural clues.

Two basic criteria were followed for the sample selection:

1. Persons closest to the suicide victim (family/friend).
2. People who lived with suicide victims for at least for last 15 days and member who continuously lived with the suicide victim.

There was no gender preference and, both male and female are taken as respondent in this study. Snow ball sampling method was adopted for conducting Thirty-five psycho-autopsies from the original sample of 242. For, maintaining the confidentiality of participants, each of them has been given a pseudo name.

Interview Setting

Thirty-five suicide cases were chosen for the study, consent was taken from the participants to pen down their interview, but before doing so, rapport formation and informal interactions with the participant was established to develop a sense of familiarity with them and make them comfortable about their participation in the study. Some opening questions were also framed during these informal sessions.

Interview Protocol

There was no fixed interview protocol for all the respondents. Order and nature of questions varied per the respondents and their life experiences. In these free floating interviews the inquiry centred on eliciting the following information:

> Each participant was interviewed for more than an hour, depending on the flow of the responses received.

1. Who were the suicide victims and what their relations with the victims were?
2. Family background and economic position of suicide victims.
3. What were the personality characteristics, daily routine of the suicide victim?
4. What were the changes (behavioural) they perceived in suicide victims in the last one month?
5. What were the incidences going on since last three months?
6. If any medical help was sought or not?

The interviews were mostly conducted at his/her room/home of the victim. Receptivity and ease of the participant for giving the interview at that point of time was assured before initiating it. As it often happens, despite the consent, often the participants did not seem relaxed enough so that the interview could be conducted. The situation was handled gently without making the participant feel uncomfortable or blocked in any sense, eventually turning it into an informal discussion.

Data Analysis and Theoretical Sampling

The first round of narratives was transcribed to code and to filter out the emerging codes and categories. Grounded theory which involves three levels of coding was used for the purpose. First level coding is a close objective analysis of the data, often line-by-line for obtaining the narrative data. Selected words, phrases, and other single units (termed as in vivo codes) of meaning are labelled as codes. This is the most basic and least abstract of the coding process. The researcher tried labelling each line, treating it as an independent indicator. This was done for all the collected interviews.

Soon after line-by-line coding second level coding which is focused coding began, which is an aggregation of first level codes into categories. As preliminary categories emerged, the researchers developed a codebook that included a list of emerging categories, preliminary descriptions of these categories, inclusion and exclusion criteria of these categories, and exemplars of text. A text unit is a part of the narrative text that represents "a meaningful point of fact, story or idea expressed by the participant" (Torill, 2006). Each category was operationally defined through the emerging codes from the transcripts.

The two main analytic activities for the study were content analysis and constant comparison method to develop the theory.

The constant comparison method is an iterative process, a back and forth process of evaluating all sources of data (e.g. transcripts, memos, literature research, expert consults) (Schreiber, 2001). Ongoing category and theoretical development occurred through intensive analysis of twelve data rich transcripts. Adequate evidence was found from the data to saturate categories and support the emerging theoretical framework.

Once categories began to form, relationships between the categories were considered. This was third level coding, also called theoretical coding, which increased in abstractness (involving relationships between categories) and generated the theory extracted from and grounded in the data. However, even at the second level coding or the development of categories, theoretical coding took place in order to generate valid categories. The goal was to develop the abstractness and breadth of the informants' realities and meanings. Crucial to effective theoretical coding and theoretical sampling was ongoing, memoing and review of memoing. Memoing, the process of making conceptual notes about the coding process, including questions, comments, and suggestions for further data collection and analysis, was conducted through the data collection and analysis phase (Schreiber, 2001). Often substantive coding (first level and some second level coding) occurred concurrently with theoretical coding (third level and some second level coding). This was part of the constant comparison and iterative processes of grounded theory.

Also, at the third level of coding the level of abstractness was more open to formulating the core category (Schreiber, 2001). Several techniques were used to facilitate the analysis. Theoretical sampling was used to refine the developing categories by exploring the indicators of defined categories till it was completely saturated leaving no further inclusion of any new indicator. Theoretical sampling included several second interviews with the selected participants. Credibility of the analysis was ensured by ongoing immersion in the data on consultation with experts in the field whereas dependability was assured by extensive memoing, theoretical and methodological discussion, and the detailed audit trail.

In the thirty-five cases which were picked up for in-depth case study and narrative analysis after completion of preliminary fieldwork there were 19 males and 16 females. According to the marital status, 15 were married, 18 unmarried and 2 were divorcee. Since, it was a random sample 16 narratives were conducted in East district, 11 from West district, 5 from South District and 3 from North district. The age group classification of the respondents can be clubbed as;, 12 belonged to the age group of 16-25, the second highest number, i.e. 9 were recorded among the 26-35 age category, 8 cases were recorded in the age group of 36-45, 4 cases were found in the age group 46-55 and only 2 narratives were recorded in the category 55 and above. Out of the 35 narratives which were conducted, 22 were residing in the rural area and 13 were residing in the urban area. In terms of educational qualification, 4 victims were illiterate (i.e. they never went to school); 3 were educated up to primary school, 10 victims went up to middle school, 4 received education upto secondary and 5 up to higher secondary. There were 5 graduates and 1 post-graduate and 2 professionally qualified victims. Monastic education was received by 1 victim.

Verma and Sachdeva (2014), in their research on 'Culture, Social Process and Suicide: A Qualitative Enquiry', identified certain major indicator which triggers the suicide behaviour separately or with interaction of another variables, as a follow-up from that study similar indicators were also used.

The meaning of indicator according to context is given below:

Table 4.1: Indicators and their definition

Category	*Indicators*	*Operational definition*
Structural level	Employment Status	It is defined in terms of whether individual is employed or not, or what kind of job they have. Nature of job they are associated with.
	Modernization	Refers to the pattern of behaviour and values based on rational, logical, and scientific against the traditional customs, ritual, and values.
	Life Style	Pattern of everyday habits associated with substance abuse (drug, alcohol) and spending free time with friend or outside the home.
	Childrearing Practices	The pattern of child rearing practices where family members giving more freedom and autonomy to the children.
	Disturbed Relationship	Define in terms of unfruitful and unpleasant relationship with family member and friends (with husband/wife, peer group, and male female friends).
	Societal Values	Societal values define in terms of Individualism (Priority for self and own family (wife, sun-daughter etc.) concern. Collectivism refers to priority given to all family (brother-sister, mother-father, uncle-aunty etc.) member living in the household than the individual; Bi-gamy, Extramarital affair etc.
	Generational Conflict	Define in terms of differences in terms of opinion, values and attitude.
Personal level	High Aspiration	Individual have high aspiration and desire in terms of materialistic orientation and leisure.
	High expectations	Individual have high expectation towards/from society family member, peer group and relative in terms of physical, emotional and economic support.
	Substance Abuse	Individual are in the habit of taking drug, alcohol etc.
	Autonomy	Refers to a person ability to think and act independently and take decision regarding oneself and other without pressure.

(Contd.)

Category	*Indicators*	*Operational definition*
	Freedom	Its power or right to act speak, think and live freely.
	Pre-Emotional Maturity	Defined in terms of emotional maturity before time. For example, individual begins to understand the aspects of physical intimacy sex, love and hate) before the age of 14 years.
Subjective experience	Isolation	Define in terms of cut-off, detach or isolated from the main stream society/family/peer group. Individual experience being isolated from society.
	Loneliness	Occurs when a person has fewer interpersonal relationships than desired or when these relationships are not as satisfying as desired. Its covers two stream emotional (absence of intimate attachment) and social (lack of friendship and network).
	Depression	Is a mental set or state of mind, where individual have state of sadness, gloom, pessimistic ideation with loss of pleasures in normally enjoyable activity, great unhappiness and hopelessness.
	Dependency for Survival	Individual experience they are dependent on another person for livelihood.
Negative Subjective experiences	Meaninglessness	Define in terms of people having no meaning, direction or purpose in his/her life.
	Worthlessness	It's a negative mindset where individual experience they are useless, do not have real value and good quality.
	Self-Esteem	Define in terms of positive and negative evaluation about own self.
	Guilt	"Feeling of responsibility or remorse for some offense, crime, wrong etc., whether real or imagined." Or its feeling of having done something wrong.
	Shame	A painful emotion or feeling caused by a strong sense of guilt, embarrassment, unworthiness, or disgrace from one's awareness that one has done something wrong or foolish.
Mediating Variable	Low Future Orientation	It is state of hopelessness where individual perceives future negatively.
	Justified Suicide Behaviour	Define in terms of individual show positive behaviour before attempt suicide in terms of pro-social, helping behaviour, fulfil his/her responsibility.
	Internal Attribution	It's a process of evaluation where individual attribute own self for any cause.

Source: Verma and Sachdeva (2014).

Table 4.1 shows the suicide instigating or mediating factors at personal level [psychological factor(s)] and at societal/structural level [Sociological factor(s)], and subjective experiential factor. Factors related to personal experiences are attributed towards, high aspiration, high expectations, substance abuse, autonomy, Illness and freedom. At structural level, the various variables are, employment status, modernization, lifestyle, childrearing practices, societal values, disturbed relationship and generational conflict are illustrated. However, in context of subjective experiences individual have feeling of isolation, loneliness, depression, and dependency for survival where as in negative subjective experience individual had feeling of meaninglessness, worthlessness, self-esteem, guilt, shame and low future orientation. In context of mediating variables: Internal attribution, justified suicidal behaviour and low level of education work as the mediating variable in suicide. Based on these factors, variables and subjective experiences the narratives have been divided into seven categories:

1. Pre-Emotional Maturity, Societal Pressure and Stigmatization.
2. Substance Abuse and Alcoholism.
3. Disturbed Relationship and Life Style.
4. High Expectation and Societal Value.
5. High Aspirations.
6. Health Problems.
7. Emotional and Behavioural problem.

Pre-Emotional Maturity, Societal Pressure and Stigmatization

Case One

The deceased was 17 years old and a student of class XI. She had a younger sister and lived with her family in Geyzing (West Sikkim). Her father was a government employee, earning approximately Rs. 45,000 per month and her mother worked at the Primary Health Centre. They were financially well off and lived in their own two storey house and had rented out one floor.

As per the friend of the deceased, the deceased was a close friend to her. As per the respondent's narration, the deceased shared almost everything with her. According to her, although her friend was very outgoing and extrovert in nature and participated in dances and co-curriculum activities at school, she had a stubborn nature, aggressive and would answer back her teachers at school which she did not approve off. She was in relationship with a boy of her class and would get extremely angry if he spoke to any other girl of the class. On the contrary, her boyfriend was of a quiet and sweet nature and would always listen to his girlfriend. He also did not have any male friends in class because he had to devote all his time to the girl. She would not even allow her friend to talk to him for too long and once when he had appreciated her, she had told her openly *"timi try na garnu... mo timi liye kut chu"* (you don't try to get close to my boyfriend, if you do, I will hit you). It was on one such occasion that her boyfriend was talking to another girl of her class, she assaulted the girl. She and her boyfriend were both suspended from school for a week because of this indiscipline; however, she was not apologetic about it. They both joined school after a week, but the boy was now not taking to her very openly, she appeared very angry and hurt as told by her friend. Her boyfriend had also shared with the friend that he is upset with the behaviour of his girlfriend and his parents are annoyed with him. She was also upset with the school authorities and her parents for not approving the relationship. On the day of suicide, a family member of the boy's family informed her family, that she had locked herself with the boy in a room and that they would not be responsible, if something happened. According to her friend, her parents had counselled her on several occasions that she was too young and marriage was not possible right now. After a few hours, the family found both of them hanging in the room. *There was a suicide note which mentioned that since, their family was not agreeing to their marriage, they did not want to live and God would unite them in heaven.* They had also expressed anger against the school authorities for suspending them and not giving them a chance to explain their point of view.

Her problem appears more of internal psychological nature than due to economic/social factors. Both the victims were going to school and were good in studies. The girl was stubborn and never apologetic about her actions. She was also extremely possessive and did not want to share her friends with anyone. The boy on the other hand was of a soft nature, but he wanted to listen to his parents after the incident at school. Her aggressive nature would not allow her to think rationally. It also appears that she must have pressurized the boy also to take such a drastic step.

Case Two

The deceased was a resident of Tashiding (West Sikkim) and was 17 years old. She was the youngest in the family. She had lost her father at a very young age and was living with her mother and brother, who was a monk; she also had a sister who was married and staying nearby. They were not economically well off; her brother was the sole earning member in the family. His earning was dependent on the seasonal prayers, rituals and festivities. She was studying in class IX at the government school.

According to the brother of the deceased, his sister was introvert by nature but being the sister of a monk and seeing all the rituals being performed at home, she also performed ritual and prayers on daily basis. She was close to her sister but did not share many things with her. She was in a relationship with a dumb boy, who was an employee of the State Government. The boy occasionally gave her gifts and sometimes money also. She was very scared to disclose about her relationship to anyone. In the mean while, she became pregnant and because of fear of stigmatization, she did not share her feeling with anyone. Her brother informed that only after she had committed suicide, did they find out that she was 7 months pregnant. On the day of the suicide she had told her sister that "I *am feeling very stressed as, I have put on lots of weight, my friends are making fun of me at school.*"

It appears from the narrative that the girl was dependent on the dumb boy economically. At the same time she was ashamed of being in relationship with a boy of unsound mind. It may also be possible that she was not aware of the fact that she was pregnant. It was learnt after going to her school that of late she had become very aloof from everyone at school, because her class mates had seen her with the boy and made fun of her, after which she had started avoiding them. Societal pressure, lack of sex education, economic depravity, stigmatization and guilt may have been the casual reasons behind her taking such drastic step.

Case Three

The deceased was 16 years old and a student of class XI and second between three siblings. She had an older sister who has completed MBBS and a younger sister who currently is in class IX. Her mother works at the university as a support staff and her father is employed at the hotel. She belonged to a middle-class family, reside in their own house and she was studying in Government school at Ranipool, Sikkim. Her parents were very conscious about educating their children and were spending money on her education.

According to the mother of the deceased, her relation with her daughter was cordial she would share things with her, she would also take care of her parents. She helped her mother in the family chores and was also very attached to her father. She was a very beautiful girl who was very caring towards her family. She was good in studies and there was no complaint from her teachers regarding her studies. Prior to her suicide, in last couple of months, she had become quiet; she would sometimes sit alone and refuse to help her mother with household work, even if her mother asked her to do so. She use to have mood swings and would get angry also. Once she asked her mother, can she marry into another caste ? Her mother had joked and said "Do you have any one in mind, I will get you married to him", to which she had replied and said "no, I do not have any one". On the day of suicide, she prepared dinner for her family members; she told her father that she wanted to prepare chicken, which her father brought. After serving food to everyone she took her plate and was eating her food very quietly in one corner. After dinner, she bid bye to her father because he worked in an evening shift at a hotel and told him to ιake care of himself "*tapai ramroo paraa jaonu", (you go safe and take care of yourself)* later she locked all the doors, ironed her school uniform and got her school bag ready. Her mother told her lets sleep together in one room today but she said *"I like to sleep alone*". Her mother asked her if she could make one phone call from her phone but she said that she did not have balance in her phone. Her mother was not feeling well that day so she gave cough syrup to her mother and made her do steam. Her mother mentioned that she was unaware about her daughter's intentions; *she looked normal but had gone quite over some months.* One early morning she was found hanging and had left a suicide note. In the note, she held no one responsible for the action she has taken. The note also contains narrative disclosure to her mother about why she has taken the drastic action. She revealed that she was in a relationship with a boy, and she is really upset about their relation as she thinks that he was seeing other girls, therefore, wants to end her life. The same has also been told to her close friend who also happens to know the boy. The friend had strongly objected both on her decision as well as the misunderstanding. The friend has told her that since the boy was a taxi driver he occasionally pick up other girls from school including herself to drop at home.

She had a lock on her phone and her mother had asked her many times to tell her the pass word, to which she had refused. Her mother mentioned that people on the day of the suicide had seen her on the roof top talking to someone for hours, her mother had also inquired what she was doing on the roof top and she had mentioned that she was talking to her elder sister, who was a doctor. People also asked her mother if she was pregnant and her mother had asked her father to go to the police and get her post-mortem report to see if she was pregnant and the police had told him that "there was not even a grain of rice in her stomach", which means that she had not eaten any food the previous night.

The narrative reveals that the individual was of an emotional nature and wanted more from her relationship. It is a case of emotional immaturity, where she could handle her feelings of love and insecurity. However, just before suicide, she was trying to create a positive image of herself, so that the family would not doubt what she was intending to do. The family had noticed behavioural changes in her, she had gone very quiet, but they were not able to anticipate that she was contemplating such an action.

Case Four

The deceased was an 18-year old, unmarried girl, who dropped from school after class VIII. She had two younger brother and sister. Her father was a school teacher and mother use to work in the ICDS centre. She was residing with her parents in Pakyong.

According to the mother of the deceased her daughter was very caring and loving by nature. She did not have many friends and dropped out of school after she failed in class IX. She had only one friend at school and she was very close to her. She was also very possessive about her and did not appreciate when her friend spoke to other students in the class. Once when her friend did not wait for her after school she became upset and was inconsolable and her teachers had to drop her home. Next day, she had, a terrible fight with her friend after which her friend stopped talking to her. She had told her mother that, that now *'primila has made boyfriends and she does not need me*'. She posted sad notes on *facebook* and on *whatsapp* according to other students of her class and then she just stopped coming to school. According to her mother she really loved her friend and did not want to share her with anyone. They also mentioned that few days before she committed suicide, she had met her friend in the market and she had come home and cried. She left a suicide note asking her parents to forgive her.

The narrative, points to the emotional and possessive nature of the victim and is more of a psychological problem than social. She had a behavioural issue and was very possessive about her friend and could not bear to share her with anyone. Rejection from her friend had made her dejected and worthless leading to suicide.

Substance Abuse and Alcoholism

Case Five

The deceased was a 50-year old man, married and a resident of East Sikkim. He dropped out of school in class IV. He lived with his parents. His wife had left him and had also taken away their son. His father was 78 years old and had a small grocery shop; this was the only means of livelihood for the family. He was able to make approximately 10,000 per month from the shop. They were living in two room rented accommodation.

According to the father of the deceased, his son was an alcoholic and a drug addict from his school days. He dropped out of school very early because of his drinking problem. He fell in love with a girl and wanted to marry her, when the girl found out that he was an alcoholic and drug addict, she left him. His father use to take him to his shop but he was never focused on work and would escape from work to drink. His parents married him and after some time he started quarrelling with his wife and soon she left him also taking away their son. His drinking continued and he sometimes used to cry and say *'my life is lost, no one loves me, and I should die....I do not have education to get a good job'*. He finally agreed to go to the rehabilitation centre and was there for two months. After he came back, he again started drinking and this time the family also started giving up on him. He told his mother "*Ab jauney time bhayeo....mailey koi maya gardeyna*' (now it is time to go...no one loves me.). On the day of suicide, he was continuously drinking and later his body was found hanging in the jungle.

This narrative explains that the deceased was not able to overcome his drug and alcohol addiction. He was aware that he was exerting economic pressure on his family and also not making any economic contributions. Lack of adequate education, failed love affair and a failed marriage were chief precipitants aggravating his problem. When he resumed consumption of alcohol after coming back from the rehabilitation centre, the apathy of his family would have made him more dejected, which is reflective by the statement "*Ab jauney time bhayeo*" (now it is time to go).

Case Six

The deceased was a 54-year old married man. He was a resident of South Sikkim. The deceased was a *lama* by profession. He had two daughters. He had lost his wife to cancer. He was living in the monastery with his two daughters. He made a living by performing ritual and prayers. His one daughter was in class IX and other in class XI.

According to his daughter, her father was a very nice man and he loved them very much and was introvert by nature. He did not have many friends and spent most of his time in prayers. He was habituated to alcohol and drank on a daily basis. In 2014, his wife was diagnosed with cancer following which she died. This episode made him very emotional and sad and he was heard saying on several occasions that *"I also want to die"*. His mental condition worsened, the family took him to the psychiatrist, but he would not take his medicines regularly. He would talk in weird manner saying *'police haru maliye khoge gardaye cha'* (police are looking for me). He would get very scared and hide in the prayer room. He did not stop drinking and according to his family made things worse for him. The other lamas at the monastery mentioned that he was a very sober person and only when he drank, his behaviour would become awkward. He once had climbed the roof of the monastery and was shouting '*we have to preserve our culture, God... someone is taking it away.*' They also mentioned that since he was the sole bread earner, he was stressed that he has to look after his family and take care of his children as they are very small. He was also in some financial debt after his wife had passed away. He would miss her a lot and drank even more. He had become mentally unstable. On the day of the suicide, he went to the monastery, brought '*chou*' (*Prasad*) and gave it to his children. He also mentioned that now he was going to play the role of both father and mother for them. He told his daughter to give him food and while she was preparing the food, he told her that he was going out. When he did not come back till late evening, on searching for him they found him hanging in jungle. Post mortem report revealed that he had been drinking before he committed suicide.

The narrative reveals that the deceased was confronted with many challenging socio-economic issues simultaneously. He was in debt after his wife passed away, he was also experiencing an emotional void, depression and loneliness had also engulfed him. His problem of alcohol consumption further aggravated his mental condition, creating some psychological symptoms in him, which is apparent from his hallucinations and words. This also reflects that despite his strong spiritual grounding, emotional issues still over powered and too the drastic step of ending his life.

Disturbed Relationship and Life Style

Case Seven

He was 22 years old, unmarried boy, a school dropout after class VIII but working in Pharmaceutical Company and earning 8,000 per month. He belonged to a Brahmin family. He was the eldest and the only son of his parents. He had two sisters who were studying in college. His father worked as a school teacher and his mother was a house wife. They were staying in a rented accommodation.

According to the mother of the deceased, he was a fun-loving person, very extrovert by nature and loved his parents and family. They only time he had disobeyed them was when he had converted to Christianity, against the wishes of his parents. He did this for his girlfriend who he loved very much and who was Christian by faith. According to his mother, although he was obsessed with her she noticed that he quarrelled a lot with the girl. The girl belonged to Namchi and couple of months before he committed suicide the girl had informed him that she was shifting to Darjeeling as she was getting a job there, this had infuriated him tremendously and he has told the girl that she should marry him. The girl had apprised him that she had recently lost her father and it would be inappropriate if she took such a step. She had also told him *that you earn so less and you will never rise because you don't have enough qualification* you will *also remain a mediocre.* The girl moved to Darjeeling and this disturbed him, he had stopped talking to his family members and had started missing work. He had mentioned to his mother, that because of his conversion to Christianity, his family had to face stigmatisation from society and he was a blot on his caste. He left a suicide note mentioning that the girl was responsible for him committing suicide and he would never forgive her. He had shared with his mother that *'he felt sad for letting down his family and hurting them'*, but he really loved the girl and wanted to marry her.

This narrative shows how the victim started feeling disturbed about his lack of higher education and his meagre salary. This point was reiterated by his girl friend who eventfully left him. He felt cheated because he had converted to Christianity because of his girlfriend. This action had hurt his parents who had to answer a lot of people in the '*samaj*'. He felt responsible for bringing a bad name to his family. He was also guilty that he had hurt the sentiment of his parents and had left him feeling despondent and dejected. All these factors combined led him to finish his life in one stroke.

Case Eight

The deceased was a 46-year-old divorcee women living with her two daughters in West Sikkim. She dropped out of school after class VI. She was a potter by profession. She was living in a one room accommodation with her children.

According to the elder daughter of the deceased, her mother was from Nepal and had an arranged marriage. She was only 14 years when she got married. Even before she got married her husband was in a relationship with another woman. The initial years of marriage were blissful for her, and she was not able to bear children for first 10 years on the marriage. After the birth of her two children, her husband became very abusive with her, he would beat her so mercilessly that once she had one to be admitted at the hospital. He would shame for giving him only daughters. She started as an occasional drinker, but gradually she started becoming habituated to it. In the meantime, her husband deserted her and moved in with other women, this was very upsetting for her and she became a chronic alcoholic. She would tell her children that her stomach hurts all the time and the pain is unbearable sometimes. She also told them, "*we don't have enough money, and I drink and waste more...but I cannot do without it.*" On the day of the suicide, she had gone to work and came back early, she prepared food for her children and told them to forgive her. She also expressed her desire to quit taking alcohol.

People have unpleasant relationships and to overcome some of the pain, they take respite in alcohol and other intoxicants. This becomes a pattern with them, aggravating their emotional condition. The deceased had an early marriage and gave birth to only daughters for which she was chastised by her husband. This is reflective of the fact how the patriarchal mindset and preference of a male child is catching up with some sections of society in Sikkim. She was economically very poor and found it difficult to support her children. She felt cheated and dejected after her husband left her for another woman. This feeling of rejection, combined with economic depravity, ill health, and alcohol addiction, resulted in her committing suicide.

Case Nine

The deceased was a 26-year unmarried boy, having his own business, belonging to West Sikkim. He was a graduate and from a well to do family and was the only son of his parents. He had two elder sisters, both were married. He lived in his two storey house. His father also helped him in the business and his mother was a house wife. He belonged to the upper caste.

According to the mother of the deceased, her son was a very bright individual full of life and was extremely close to her. He was also humble by nature, sensitive and would get very emotional about the problems of other. He would try his best to help them in some way or the other. He was very close to his family members and his sisters. His parents wanted to marry him but he was in a relationship with married women, who was a divorcee, she belonged to Scheduled Caste and was also a mother. He did not inform any of his family members about this relation, but they learnt about it from his friends, and confronted the girl and told her that, their son was still not settled and they would not accept a woman with a child to be their daughter-in-law, who belonged to a low caste. After this the woman, had called him up and told him that it was very wrong on his part to share everything with his family members and now she would not be a part of his life. According to his mother, this divorcee lady did not have a good character and was deserted by her husband because of her amorous activities. She had given a sad story to her son and was extracting money from him. They were also having a physical relation. After being rejected by the woman he had become very quiet, he was very emotional by nature and felt that the woman needed him and he was not able to extend her any help. On one occasion he saw another man leaving her house and when he had asked her who he was, she had reprimanded him saying it was none of his business. He had told his mother, *that "mailey tapey ko kura sune na, tapaie theek he thiyeo (I did not listen to you, you were right)."* His parents were looking for a girl for him to marry. On the day of suicide, he had gone to meet the lady and she had refused to meet him. He left a suicide note for his parents mentioning that he was sorry for his action.

The narrative revealed that the individual was emotional by nature and an altruist. He was touched by the hardship the married woman was facing and he wanted to help her. The woman belonged to the low caste and her marital status was causing a lot of problem for his parents. However, after the relationship was disclosed to his parents, the reaction of the woman had hurt him tremendously and he felt cheated. He was also facing criticism from society for his actions, but he was truly in love with the woman. Rejection in love and his helplessness for not being able to support the woman increased his despondency and he started keeping himself aloof. Failure in relationship and shame he had brought to his family because of being involved with low caste, married woman and ultimately being rejected by her made him very emotionally vulnerable. Social factors of caste, strong parental disapproval followed by rejection resulted in suicide.

Case Ten

The deceased was an unmarried 25-year old girl, working as a Post-graduate teacher in West Sikkim. By virtue of being a post graduate teacher, she was earning very well. She had two sisters and two brothers and was the middle sister. She had lost her mother when she was very young. Her elder sister was married and both the brothers were working out of the state. She lived alone with her father in West Sikkim. She belonged to the Brahmin community.

According to her younger sister, she shared a very warm relationship with her sister. Her sister was very beautiful and attractive girl. She was working as a Post-graduate teacher in West Sikkim and was engaged to be married to her boyfriend. She was extremely popular among her students for her beauty, good nature, and friendliness. The deceased was in a relationship for a very long time, with the boy and she was getting married. She sometimes use to share with her sister that she finds him quite boring and he keeps checking on her whereabouts all the time. In her school where she was working there was another male colleague with whom she shared a very nice relationship and she was also in love with him. This boy also loved her, but she did not apprise him about her engagement and marriage plans. Her fiancée learned about her affair from some other people and he called her to meet him. When she met him, he threw all her things from his house and told her that she did not exist for him. She was very hurt and when she went back to her male colleague he told her *"if you cannot be true to your lover, how can you be true to me, I don't want you in my life, you can go back."* After this incident, she became very sad, she stopped dressing up nicely and eating her food. She told her friends at school, that she is suffering from some disease which is making her very sad. Her friends told her to go and check by the doctors, but she said it looks like an incurable disease.

On the day of suicide she called up her fiancée and told him that she really loved him and missed him, to which he had responded saying *"you are a characterless girl, I don't even care if you die"*. She had mentioned this to her younger sister. She left a suicide note in which he had mentioned that because she is suffering from an incurable disease, she is ending her life and that no one is responsible for her death. She feared stigmatization from society and her lover at school also spoke ill of her this disturbed her tremendously. She wrote a suicide note blaming it on sickness so that her family would be spared of shame.

The narrative reveals that the deceased feared stigmatization from society. She even believed that now her chances of marriage are grim as and her lovers would talk about her in society. Her high caste status and close proximity within the caste members further increased her fears. To save her family from the ignominy she wrote a suicide note blaming sickness for her actions. She had been deserted by her fiancée and she could not gather the courage to tell her family members. She was confused in her relationship. She loved both the boys and rejection by them had made her very despondent.

Case Eleven

The deceased was a 38-year old married woman and a resident of North Sikkim. She worked as a constable in the police department. Her husband was a taxi driver and 28 years old. She resided alone in a two-room rented accommodation. Her parents lived in Dzongu, she had two brothers who were agriculturists.

According to the friend of the deceased, she was a very nice natured person and very dedicated to her work. All her seniors were very fond of her as she was very efficient professionally. She supported her family financially and since her brothers were married and having children, she felt she had more responsibility towards them. She had received a lot of marriage proposals in the past, but she had always turned them down. Her friend was very surprised when she had told her that she had got married to a boy who was ten years younger than her and was a taxi driver. Everyone was surprised, how on her rank and status, she could marry such a low status person. She seemed very happy and had given a party in the '*thana*' (police station). She had shared with her friend that her family was not happy with this marriage because her husband did not belong to her community. A few months after marriage, she suffered a miscarriage and was hospitalized, she shared with her friend that she was not aware that her husband takes drugs and alcohol and after their marriage, he also stopped working and would start drinking from the morning. The deceased, was constantly made fun off by her aquittances, that she had married a boy of her sons age. Her husband would keep asking her for money and one day she learnt that he had another wife in Gangtok, they had a big fight over this issue. She was very disturbed that day, she told her colleague at the police station, *now I understand why people commit suicide, it takes away so much of the pain and sorry*. She was found hanging in the jungle. She had left a suicide note where he had mentioned that, she hoped ending her life would end her problems.

The narrative explains the pain the victim was feeling after being betrayed in love. On finding about his earlier marriage she felt betrayed and cheated and was unable to cope with the shock. She had rebelled and revolted against the norms of the society and married a man of a different community who was younger than her in the hope to get love and affection.

High Expectation and Societal Value

Case Twelve

The deceased was a 20-year old Nursing student residing in Gangtok. She had an elder brother. Her parents were both working as Government Employee. She came from a financially well to do family. They stayed in a rented accommodation in Gangtok, and belonged to South Sikkim.

According to the brother of the deceased, his sister was very close to him and shared all her feelings with him. She was interested in singing and was also very fond of sketching. She had a lot of friends and would often go and spend time with them. She was a fun-loving girl and full of energy. The incident that upset her was that she was caught cheating by her teachers during the examinations. She tried to convince her teachers and tell them that she was being wrongly framed. She told her brother that *'I have not done it, I feel very sad.'* According to her, it was the only incident that had disturbed her, otherwise she was very happy and was good in her studies. On the day of the suicide, she had gone to college and later that evening she hanged herself.

The narrative reveals that the deceased had expectations from herself; she strongly believed in values of honesty and was disturbed after she was chastised for cheating. This incident had scarred her and had affected her psyche. Since she was a good student, she felt this action was going to affect her academic progress and achievement. She was unable to face her teachers her friends and could not face the humiliation opting for the drastic step.

Case Thirteen

The deceased was 21 years old and a resident of Gangtok. He was the only child of his parents and after his father passed away; his mother was running the house. His mother was a government employee. He dropped out of school after class VIII. They lived in their own residence, a humble three room house.

According to the mother of the deceased, her son had a quiet nature and hardly spoke to her or anyone else. He was not very good in studies and after he failed in class XI, he left his studies. He later, left for Qatar in the Middle-East to look for a job. After he returned from Qatar, he had little conversation, shared less of his experiences and feelings with his mother and family members. Whenever, he went to visit his relatives and other family members on some holidays and festivals, the relatives would tell him that since he was the only son, he should help his mother. In the earlier years of dropping out of school he was involved in an accident, because of which he had developed a limp in his leg. After his accident, he had told his mother *'I am sorry, that I have never helped you, I feel very useless... and now I have a broken leg also.'* Half a month earlier to his death he had started working as a courier delivery boy for some agency. His mother mentioned that, this job was also acquired with favours from her friends, after he started to work he would come home late and sometimes even drunk, his mother doubted that he was into contrabands, she thinks it was his company that led him to do all those things as he spent most of his time with his friends. On the day of the suicide, he was very drunk and had not gone to work; he told his mother that he wanted to sleep.

This narrative explains that the social pressure which the victim experienced after dropping out of school, he had anticipated to be successful in his overseas venture in the middle east, but after his accident, he started suffering from body shaming. He also felt that he was not fulfilling his duties as a son and was a burden on his mother. He also felt that he was unsuccessful and needed the help of others to achieve anything in life. This aggravated despondency and low self-esteem must have resulted in committing suicide.

Case Fourteen

The deceased was a 16-year old student studying in class VII in South Sikkim. He was the only child of his parents. His parents worked as government employees. They lived in a rented accommodation and had all the daily amenities for a comfortable life.

According to the mother of the deceased, he was very close to her. He always shared everything with both his parents and made big plans for future. He told his mother he wanted to become a computer engineer and work in USA. He was a very bright student and was also very good in computers. He helped everyone in the neighbourhood if they needed any help in computers or internet. Once there was a complaint from his teachers that he was showing pornography films to the students of his class and he had created secret files on the school computer where he had saved objectionable material. He was suspended from school for a week because of this action. At home his parents also confiscated his phone and laptop. He told his parents that he was innocent and he did not open any such files on the computer, advertisements prop up when one works on the computer and one of his friends opened it and since he is good in computers the blame came on him. His parents had gone to inform the school about this, but the school authorities mentioned that he would not be allowed to attend school for one week. After this incident, he became very quiet, his parents gave his laptop back to him, but he would never open it. He was very unwilling to go to school and even missed his class test. He got hospitalized for dehydration and weakness and after he returned from the hospital, he became quitter. He had told his mother, *now I can never become a computer engineer, I feel scared to touch the computer*. On the day of the suicide, he opened his laptop and that had made his parents happy. After doing something on it for few hours, he closed it and told his mother that he was going to sleep. He committed suicide by hanging himself and his Face book status said... *me innocent... bye.*

The narrative highlights the rejection and shame which the victim suffered after he was caught in School. Since he was very good in studies, he felt this incident had scarred his life for ever, teachers and students commented on him and he felt he had brought a bad name to his family. He was unable to bear the shame and despite his best efforts to prove himself innocent, the school authorities did not believe him. He was unable to cope with this shame and committed suicide.

Case Fifteen

The deceased was a 27-year old unmarried girl residing in Gangtok. She had passed class X, but dropped out of school after she failed in class XI. She was originally from Kalimpong, but was working in Gangtok. Her father was a potter and her mother was a daily wage earner. She had two younger brother and sister.

According to the friend of the deceased, her friend was not off a very extrovert nature and had few friends. She had met her when they had started working in a private company at Gangtok. She spent a lot of her time on her phone and was very fond of taking selfies.

She was from Kalimpong and according to her friend she was earlier married but she had not disclosed this to anyone in the workplace. She was very young and had eloped with a boy and had left him after a few months because he was not earning enough. In her family back home her father was a potter and her mother also worked as a daily wage earner, but she did not share this information with anyone. She was a very beautiful girl and would take care of her looks and almost spent her entire money on clothes and buying cosmetics. *She projected herself as belonging to a very rich family.* She hardly ate anything and was seen munching on Wi-Wi (a variety of chips) and was often with a bottle of water. Her friend never saw any food items in her house and they often joked that since you spend everything on your looks you do not have any money left to eat. Some months before she committed suicide, she had developed black patches on her face and was very frequently visiting the dermatologist. According to her friend she spent hours in front of the mirror and posted a lot of pictures on face book and would get very happy to see the number of likes she would get on those pictures. She was not in a stable relationship, but had male friends who would visit her room. She always told her friend *'mo dhani manchi sangha byae garne'* (I want to marry a rich man). Few days before the suicide she had shared with her friend that now *she was not pretty anymore and this was troubling her.* She once told her friend *'I feel like scrubbing my face off, I want to cut my neck'*. A week before she committed suicide, she had gone for a birthday party and some friends had posted some pictures and she did not get enough likes and she was feeling very sad. On the day of the suicide she had taken leave from office and had gone to the beauty parlour. She had even posted pictures on *facebook* saying Naina—*the gorgeous.* She had spoken to her family and her friends that she was tired and she wanted to sleep and that she was switching her phone. She committed suicide by hanging herself.

The narrative explains the victim's obsession with herself. It is an example of the addiction and dependence of the youth on social media. They have the desire to project them as affluent, beautiful and receive appreciations from everyone. The deceased was ashamed of her family background and would not share details about her personal life with anyone, she left her husband because he was not earning enough and did not share this with anyone. She was filling the vacuum of her life by keeping herself busy on *facebook* and social media. This narrative also highlights, how the young generation has become disconnected with reality and lives in a virtual world which if tampered has a bad effect on their psyche.

Case Sixteen

The deceased was a 43-year old Engineering graduate from North Sikkim. He was the only son of his parents, had an elder sister who was married. His family was financially well off and his father was working with the State Government before he expired. After his death, his mother was living off the pension. They had two more houses in Gangtok, from which they collected rent.

According to the sister of the deceased her brother was a jovial person and always studied in the hostel. After he was selected in Engineering, he never came back to Sikkim and was working outside the state in Delhi. After his mother fell ill, he was asked to come back because his father had recently passed away. After coming back from Delhi, he was looking for a job but because of his age he was not getting a government job. Since his family was financially well off, they asked him to start a business and get married. His sister mentioned that he was not very happy after coming back from Delhi. He felt the people in Sikkim did not have the right exposure and were only running after constructing houses. He even told his mother, that she should come and stay with him in Delhi instead of him moving here. After coming back from Delhi, he developed blood pressure problem and frequently complained of stomach ache. He had been diagnosed with liver cirrhosis and was under treatment. A few weeks before he committed suicide, he called up his sister and told her that he was going back and that he was feeling very wasted here. *'Even the internet does not work properly here, how do you all live here he had told his sister.'* On the day of the suicide he had gone to the bank and settled all the accounts and took out a print out of all the statements and gave his mother to keep. He signed all the cheque books and told his mother that he will not eat food today and he was going to watch a movie and that she should take care of herself. He later hanged himself that night. He left a suicide note in which he wrote that *life was hard and he did not feel too well to help his mother and he was becoming a burden on her.*

The narrative highlights the turmoil the victim was facing between his duties as a son and his own expectations from life. He was facing an acculturation stress after coming back to his traditional society after spending many years in the metropolitan city. He also did not want to fail in his duties as a son, but felt that he was not doing justice to his mother or himself. This role conflict was putting unnecessary pressure on him, resulting in him ending his life.

High Aspirations

Case Seventeen

The deceased was a 27-year old man who worked as a contractor in West Sikkim. He was the only son of his parents and he had an elder sister who was married. He studied up to class X and then started working as a contractor. He lived in his own house with his parents, which he had very tastefully constructed.

According to the sister of the deceased, her brother was a responsible son to his parents and performed his duties and services for the family with utmost sincerity. He loved her a lot and was a good uncle to her children. He helped her financially and always carried a lot of gifts when he went to visit her. However, his relationship with his wife was not cordial and they would frequently quarrel with each other. He was very loyal to his wife, but at the same time he was also very possessive. He doubted that his wife was having an affair with some as she was constantly talking to someone on the phone. He had tried to hang himself twice, but was saved by his family members. According to his sister, his wife was in a relationship but she always lied. She painted a different picture of herself in front of his parents and use to hit him in private. After his two attempts to commit suicide his wife left him and started living with her parents, this had upset him, but on the counselling on his parents he had started his work again. One day he was called by his in-laws that his wife was expecting a child, and since the child was his he should take his wife back. This was not acceptable to him, but after a lot of pressure from both the families he brought his wife home. He would share with his sister that, his relationship with his wife is not congenial and he feels *"very trapped"*. Before he committed suicide, there was a change in his nature, he had gone quitter and would say *"life has not treated me right"*.

The narrative reveals that the victim was not happy in his relationship and he was suffering from depression which is apparent from his earlier two suicide attempts. His problem had got internalized and, he felt a failure in life and felt no one understood him and forced him to be with his wife who was not loyal to him. He was also not sure that the child was his and felt cheated trapped. The apathy of his wife and her parents troubled him. He was having behavioural issues and rejection worsened his condition, resulting in him committing suicide.

Case Eighteen

The deceased was a 40-year old married woman residing in West Sikkim. She was married 8 years ago and had a 5-year old son. She had an elder brother who was also married. Her husband was an agriculturist worker and had his own piece of land. She lived in her own house and would accompany her husband to work. Her father was a '*jhakri*' (Faith healer), she had lost her mother when she was 20 years old.

According to the husband of the deceased, they had been married 8 years before and everything was good in their marriage. She was a very caring and devoted wife and also socially maintained good relations with everyone in the neighbourhood. Suddenly, after 8 years she started behaving mentally unstable. Her behaviour would fluctuate according to the new moon/full moon, rest of the time her behaviour would be normal. Her husband took her to the doctor and they were treating her for mental illness. She, however, did not show any signs of improvement and her blood pressure also starting fluctuating. Later her husband took her to the faith healers and he informed him that your wife is going to become a *'mata' (Spirit possession/Goddess)* and hence after performing some rituals he proclaimed her as a *'mata'* and told her that she should not have got married. She told her husband, that since *she was daughter of a Jhakri it was correct and now higher forces will take revenge from her for getting married and not following the commands*. The faith healer told her husband that since she is a '*mata'* she should not have married and this was the reason for her unstable mental health condition. According to her husband, her condition deteriorated further after this. She started blaming her husband for their marriage, she became rude with her child and her behaviour became very stubborn, if anyone in the family did anything against her wishes, she would become very angry and say *'I will commit suicide'*.

Her husband mentioned that she was having a lot of behavioural issues and somehow her revelation of being a *mata*, put a lot of pressure on her. On the day of the suicide she told her family members that it is Diwali time and she was going to play *'Baileni'* (group of young girls singing songs, who come and give blessings to the family members during Diwali, this ritual is cultural specific to the Nepali community). She also told her husband that she had important things to discuss with *'them'* and when he had asked her who is this *'them'* she said, I cannot tell you. Later her husband found out that she did not go anywhere and her body was found hanging in the jungle.

This case shows that sometimes individuals when aspiring for spiritual growth suffer from this dilemma, in making a choice between the material and spiritual world putting stress on them. The narrative reveals the flux in the mind on the deceased the revelation that she was meant for a higher purpose in life and because of her marital status this was not possible, had created a lot of confusion in her mind.

Case Nineteen

The deceased was a 35-year old married man and a faith healer by profession. He belonged to West Sikkim. His father was also a faith healer and he had inherited it. His wife was a housewife and he had no child. He had never been to school and his economic condition was good.

According to the brother of the deceased, his brother was a faith healer *(Bijwa)* of the Subba Community. He was very close to his elder brother and use to discuss all important matters with him. By virtue of being a *Bijwa,* he was frequently invited by community members for conducting rites and rituals. Financially he was earning enough, but he always complained that he was not able to excel in his profession, he wanted and dreamt of being a celebrated *Bijwa* of his community. He always complained that I do only *'sano sano phuk phak', hamroo bao kasto gyane thiyo* (small irrelevant shamanistic rituals, forwarding spirits and I am not able to accomplish anything big our father was such a great faith healer). According to his brother, when a person becomes a *Bijwa,* he goes into an altered state of consciousness, which makes a person appear as mentally unstable. He was not able to fathom that his brother was becoming mentally unstable and he was convinced that his brother was trying to achieve a new dimension in his shamanistic practices. On the day of the suicide he told his brother that today he was going to perform and invite spirits and ask them for guidance. After he committed suicide, his brother felt that may have been possessed during the ritual and committed suicide (*Sihao Lageko*). His brother also apprised that after he passed away, his body was treated as impure and it was not taken inside the house, because he had committed suicide. He felt sad for his brother and felt that somewhere his aspirations to make it into a big *Bijwa* were responsible for him committing suicide.

The narrative reveals that the deceased had high aspiration of becoming a great faith healer. Since he had inherited it from his father, it was a legacy he wanted to carry it forward. He always compared himself with his father and felt he was not good enough. The societal pressure of excelling as faith healer and failure to achieve his dreams resulted in a conflict in his mind, encouraging him to take this step towards suicide.

Case Twenty

The deceased was a 36 year old man from East Sikkim. He was the youngest among three siblings. He came from a well to do family but he dropped out of school very early after class V. He did not have any children. He had a government job, which was given to him after his away father had passed, in service.

According to the wife of the deceased, her husband was a simple man. He was suffering from epilepsy from his childhood because of which he had to drop-out of school. This suffering had made him an introvert and he did not have close friends. He use to discuss with his wife that "*mero sabpaye saathi ramro kardeyecha... mo matri istu chu*" (all my friends are doing well in life I am only left unsuccessful). He also use to share with his wife that people make fun of me and think that I am *'mental'*. However, he was not a regular with his medication and would generally miss them if not reminded by his wife. He was also a habituated drinker and because of this drinking problem he also missed going to work. He would sometimes drink for days together and then he would get the epilepsy attack which would make him very weak. He once got some a major wound in his right leg which gradually spread to his other leg also. The wound had a bad stench as a result of which people stopped coming near him. His wife however did not leave him and continued to care for him. One day he asked his wife to make love with him, to which she refused because the wounds on his legs were bleeding. After this episode he became very angry and emotional, he slapped his wife and yelled at her. His drinking increased more after this episode and he stopped communicating with his wife. On the day of the suicide, his father in law had come to visit him, and he had told him that he was sorry and that he was a failure. His father in law told him that he will take him to Siliguri for treatment and after that he would recover... to which he had agreed. Later, that evening when his wife had gone to visit the neighbours, he hanged himself.

The narrative highlights that prolonged sickness made the victim emotional and despondent. He suffered from a sense of worthlessness and whenever he was sick his inferiority complex would further increase. When he physically abused his wife in a fit of anger he became very guilty and that incident pushed him towards committing suicide.

Case Twenty-one

The deceased was a 24-year old unmarried woman and a resident of East Sikkim. She belonged to a very affluent family. She had one elder brother and one younger sister. Her father and mother were Government employee, they are a well placed family and also politically connected.

According to the brother of the deceased he shared a very affectionate relationship with his sister. Everyone really appreciated her because she was very good academically and always got good scores in school and college. She had finished her M.Sc. from Sikkim University and wanted to get enrolled into Ph.D. She did not get through the Ph.D., but she told her brother that she would try again. She was very scared after she was diagnosed with tuberculosis, but with the support of her family and good treatment she recovered. During 2015, she was again diagnosed with MDR-TB (Multi-drug resistant-tuberculosis). With support from her family members, her treatment started, but she often complained that these medicines are making her irritable and she wanted to discontinue them. Her family supported her and even took her to the psychiatrist, who mentioned that, this was happening because of the medication. In the mean time she told her family members that she wanted to go to UK to study to which they agreed, but told her that since it was a 14 months course of the medication, she could leave after she had finished her treatment.

In the meanwhile her behaviour was changing and she would tell her family members that because of my sickness, I will have a lot of problem in my passport also, I will not be able to go. *"I will never get cured, I really wanted to make it big in life, and my other friend is already ahead of me."* She was also very fragile constitutionally and the prolonged sickness was further making her weak. She felt her mind could not register anything and her memory was failing her. She left a suicide note mentioning that she would never recover and her dreams are all shattered, she would ask God for a better body and come back.

The narrative reveals that, the victim wanted to be very successful in her life. She had big dreams and wanted to go abroad for higher education. However, prolonged sickness was shaking her self-confidence and she felt she was being pushed away from her dreams. The relapse of the disease further alienated her and the accompanying depression with it would have pushed her to taking her own life. The case also highlights the psychosis which occurs after taking drugs for MDR-TB and these needs to be treated for many patients.

Case Twenty-two

The deceased was 40-year old unmarried man from Gangtok, East Sikkim. He had an elder brother who is a secretary rank officer. He was a graduate from Delhi University and was working as an LDC, with the state government. He was staying with his brother in his house, his father was a retired state government official and had recently died.

According to the brother of the deceased, his brother was very friendly in nature and lots of friends, after office he would spend most of his time with his friends. He was unmarried and always told his brother 'girls take away your freedom, your life'. Once he would become very quiet and sit in his room. He felt life had given him a raw deal. All his friends had qualified the under secretary examination and now were in good positions, but *he had not made it big*. He once told his brother after coming back from a party '*my friends are doing so well, life has cheated me'. Even you have done well for yourself and I have not made it.* A few days before he committed suicide, he told his brother that he wanted to marry and that he was seeing someone and she was an under secretary. His brother had laughed and said *do you think she will marry you*? On the day of the suicide he was drinking at home, which was very unusual and he had also vomited in the washroom twice. He kept murmuring something which no one could understand. His brother had tried to talk to him but he said that he was fine and this was the last time he was doing it. When his brother woke up in the morning he saw his brother lying dead in the room.

It appears from the narrative that structural and personal level factors exert pressure on individuals increasing subjective feelings of worthlessness. Everyone in the family of the deceased was well placed and he felt a misfit. After he fell in love with a girl, the fear of rejection was always in his mind. It may be that he had broken up from his girl friend and again he was blaming is professional incompetence and position as the reason behind it. His employment status was not per his expectation, increasing his inferiority complex. His problem was more from high aspirations and expectations from his life and not being able to strike a balance between them.

Health Problems

Case Twenty-three

The deceased was a 40-year old married/separated woman and was living with her two children—daughter and son in Gangtok. She dropped out of school after class VIII as the family did not have enough money and both the parents died early and she and her sister were raised by relatives. She had her small business which she jointly shared with her sister. She had only one younger sister, who was unmarried. She lived in West Sikkim.

According to the sister of the deceased, her sister was a very hard working person, caring and very loving by nature. She was a patient of depression for some time, but was not under any medication. She would go to the doctor when her children forced her and once she would come back she would not take the medicine. According to her sister, she was disturbed from her married life, she had been deserted by her husband after the birth of her two children and 6 years after her marriage. Her husband was now living with his second wife in Gangtok. She had started drinking and sometimes would drink for days. Her children and sister would hide about her condition from everyone, because they did not want their mother to earn a bad name. She was close to her sister, and really loved her children. They told her many times not to drink since the alcohol aggravated her depression, but she would not listen to anyone. On the day of the suicide she told her sister that she had met her husband and he looked very happy and he behaved as if he did not recognize her. She was drinking that entire day and had locked herself in the room. When her children had knocked on the door, she had said that she was fine and would overcome. But when she did not open the door, they had to break in and found her hanging.

From the narrative it appears that the victim was a patient of depression but suffered an emotional loss after her husband left her for other woman. She had suffered a lot since her childhood and being the elder of the two sisters she had struggled in her childhood because of her family circumstances. Her depression worsened after frequent consumption of alcohol. This is a case of bigamy, dropout and taking respite in alcohol to ease pain. It is scientifically proven that alcohol has a depressing effect on senses, aggravating symptoms of a clinically depressed Individual.

Case Twenty-four

The deceased was a 30-year old married woman, and resident of Ranipool, East Sikkim. She was married 8 years ago and had one daughter. She was a housewife and the only child of her parents. She dropped from school after class VIII. Her husband was a taxi driver, but he had his own taxis and they were financially well to do.

According to her husband, his wife was a person who loved life and loved herself. She was very close to her family members including her husband. She was a very smart lady and who could get anything done because she spoke very politely and nicely to everyone. She participated in religious activities and took good care of her family members, however, after the death of her father she became a quite person. She continued to do all the household chors, but the love and affection was missing. Her husband tried very hard to help her in whatever way he could but she use to say "*I hear sounds of birds, they are telling me that my father is calling me.*" When he took her to the market, she would get very frightened with the sounds of the cars and taxis. She told her husband "*I want to lie on the road so that a car can kill me.*" On the day of suicide, she told her husband that she is having a lot of anxiety and chest pain, she wanted to drink chicken soup. Her husband told her that she should lie down and rest and in the meanwhile he will go and fetch chicken. When her husband came back he found her hanging there was a suicide note which said that *"my father has come in a car to take me and I am going, I have prepared the soup for you."*

It appears from the narrative that the death of the father of the victim had made her emotionally vulnerable; she may have been suffering from depression which the family was not able to decipher. She was hallucinating and was unable to control her emotions. By virtue of being the only child, she may have been pampered and the loss of her father, resulted in collapse of her support system. Although, her husband really loved her, he was not able to compensate for her father.

Case Twenty-five

The deceased was a 17-year-old girl and a student of class XI studying in Ranipool, East Sikkim. She had an elder brother and lived with her parents. Her father was self-employed and her mother was housewife. They were not financially well off and lots of money was spent on the treatment of the deceased, adding to their debt.

According to the mother of the deceased, she shared a nice relation with her daughter. Her daughter was quite introvert by nature and was suffering from a heart problem but it could not be diagnosed properly. She actively participated in all social activities associated with her community or *samaj*. Because of her sickness she use to get tired very fast and many a times she use to complain that *'mero heart karda, mo key karnoo sakdey na'* (Because of my heart I cannot do so many things). Her mother also consoled her that she would get fine, but she also worried about the finances and told her mother '*mero jeevan kamti cha* (I have a short life)'. Few days, prior to her suicide she had gone to attend a Ramnavmi mela and after that she could get out of bed for a few days. After this she looked very pale and became quitter. Her mother felt that some evil spirits had taken away her daughter *'Sihaa lageko hola'*. She felt she had a small life only '*Lekhata mai tei hola'* (her life was only written short).

The narrative revealed that the victim was dejected because of her sickness; she also felt her sickness was creating an economic pressure for her parents. She felt she was a liability for her family and by ending her life she felt she could reduce the problems of her parents. Her problem was more physiological and the high cost of the treatment was putting pressure on her family. Ending her life, would end her ordeal and also the family

Case Twenty-six

The deceased was a 56-year old man residing in West Sikkim. He never attended school and was a farmer by profession. He belonged to the BPL category. He had two children a daughter and a son. His wife also helped him in the field, but they were not able to generate enough money. They were very weak financially and lived in one room rented accommodation.

According to the wife of the deceased, the family belonged to the BPL category (Below Poverty Line) and they were very poor. First their daughter came down with MDR-TB (Multi Drug Resistant Tuberculosis) and later her husband contacted the diseases from his daughter. Everyone told him that you have got this disease because you are poor and that really troubled him. He was cured from MDR, but often told his wife that the high doses of the medication make him very irritable. He often sat alone in his field looking at the sky. In the meantime his daughter who was suffering from MDR died, this made him very sad. He would often travel to different places talking to people, how he could get cured and often came back saying that we don't have the money. Six months before he committed suicide he was admitted to the hospital, but he kept complaining that these medicines are making him very irritable. He often told his son that '*justo lekheko huncha. tusto he huncha*' (whatever my fate is, that only will happen). After he was discharged from the hospital, he would say that his daughter is calling him, she is all alone and she needs someone to talk to. The family took him to a faith healer and he had told them '*keya lage ko cha'* (he been possessed by something). On the day of the suicide, he took a bath, wore clean clothes, he consumed food more than usual and told his wife that he is going to the field, when he did not come back in the evening, they went to search for his and found him hanging in the cowshed.

The narrative highlights that economic depravity and sickness pushes the individual in the vicious circles of dejection and self harm. The loss of his daughter and his inability to save his daughter made him very helpless driving him to suicide.

Case Twenty-seven

The deceased was a 54-year old government employee and worked as a school teacher. His wife was also working as a school teacher and was a graduate. He had two daughters, both of them were married. The family was financially good and lived in their own house in South Sikkim.

According to the wife of the deceased, they had been married for 26 years and were happy in their marriage. He, however, always felt that is wife was cheating on him and every time she saw her talking on the phone, he felt either she was talking to her lover or complaining about him to her family members. He was not initially like this, it was only after 2014 when he met with an accident and fractured his spine because of which he developed a limp in his leg that he started becoming suspicious of his wife. He also felt his children also made fun of him and he would scold them. Both his children were married and were not staying with him. A few months before he committed suicide, his wife had called up the children mentioning that their father had given her a beating and had broken her leg. The children had come and taken their mother away after this incident. However, their mother came back after some time because she really loved her husband. Things were well for a few days then one night when his wife woke up feeling suffocated *she saw her husband pressing her neck* and trying to kill her. After this he was taken to the psychiatrist, but he would not improve. He hanged himself in the bathroom and he had gone very quite before the suicide.

The narrative explains the inferiority complex and the negative state of mind of the victim that he developed after his injury. Since he was living with his wife, he started suffering from mis-apprehensions that his wife would leave him. He was concocting and hallucinating that people were conspiring against him. It appears that he suffered not only from a physical set back but also a mental set back. He had also developed some psychiatric problem, which despite treatment did not help him.

Case Twenty-eight

The deceased was a 25-year old unmarried boy from Bihar but had been born and brought up in Sikkim. His father had a small shop in

Ranipool and he assisted his father in the shop. He had a younger brother and elder sister who was married.

According to the father, his son was a healthy boy and assisted his father in the shop. He was very committed to his work. Once he went to attend a funeral of his friend and after that he fell sick. He started becoming very sick and was always saying that spirit were calling him and asking him to commit suicide. Parents were quite devastated and believe that he committed suicide because some spirit was asking him to do. There were others in the village who also believed that spirits ask people to commit suicide.

It appears from the narrative that the victim might have suffered from some kind of fear after attending the funeral and may have been emotionally affected as the funeral of his friend was off. This may have been exaggerated by others in the society that he might have become possessed. It was a common belief among individuals in society that evil spirits invite people to commit suicide, it may just be case of some psychological disorder which because of the prevailing belief of superstitions in the society could not be diagnosed resulting in the individual committing suicide.

Emotional and Behavioural Problem

Case Twenty-nine

The deceased was a resident of Ravanagla (South Sikkim). She was 63 years old and third among five siblings. Her husband was an agricultural worker and along with that he ran a small grocery shop. She had three children, two daughters and one son. She was a housewife and would occasionally go and work in her small field. She never attended school but her children had taught her to write her name.

According to the daughter of the deceased, who was a 38-year old woman and was working in Gangtok. Her mother was very emotional by nature. She was very attached to her father and after his death started consuming alcohol. Her family was very supportive and they wanted her to quit alcohol. She started to develop a skin problem which may be because of her alcohol consumption. She became very upset because of this. She was a beautiful women and use to take pride in her beauty, but after her skin problem started she further became dejected and started drinking more. After the loss of her father when she was still trying to recover, her husband suddenly passed away after 5 months suddenly. After this shock her drinking increased and she started looking and behaving mentally unstable, she would say her father and husband are calling her. She would iron the clothes of her husband and say he has come and has to go to work. She was very close to her daughter but, even her emotional support was not able to give her strength. She told other on several occasions that she was not a good mother and was not discharging her duties properly. On the day of suicide, she told her daughter *"That I want to be born beautiful again and I don't want to drink anymore and I promise to try to quit from today."*

Here the problem is more internal psychological and not due to environmental or economic factors. It may be inferred that the because of the deceased emotional nature, she was not able to handle the loss of her father and husband. She may have been depressed after these losses occurred in her life and she started consuming alcohol. This may have aggravated her psychological condition. She prided in being beautiful and when she developed a skin problem, it was another blow to her self-confidence. She felt guilty about not being able to discharge her duties properly as a mother and was also guilty about her drinking problem, but found it difficult to quit.

Case Thirty

The deceased was 23 years old and a resident of Bihar, but had been residing in Sikkim from birth. He dropped out of school after class VIII School. He lost his father when he was 10 years old. His mother had a grocery shop in the heart of Rangpo bazaar and was doing well for herself. He had an elder sister, who was married in Bihar.

According to the mother of the deceased, her son was weak in studies and also physically weak (stomach problems), because of which he dropped out of school. He did not help her mother in the shop and roamed around with friends and always asked money from her. Since he was the only child she had after her daughter got married, she also gave him lots of money. He was close with his mother and some of his friends, the recreational activities he was involved in was cricket he had played a quite a number of cricket tournaments and was well known. His friend circle being big he participated in lots of local activities and helped people in need, since he was always away from home he was never present in the religious functions that was conducted at home, even if he was present he did not take any interest in participation in the rituals. He had left a note mentioning about his love for a girl from Pakyong, but they had some problem in the relationship and she was cheating on him and the fight led to his breakup with her. He had caught her with some other guy and it led to a huge fight with her. The note also mentioned that since he was a Bihari and an outsider she did not want to be with him. He was also into contrabands, he took un-prescribed drugs. His mother also had the knowledge of him taking these substances.

From this narrative, it is clear that the individual did not have any vision about his life. Here the problem is more because he dropped out of school and never focused on any achievement. He had also become a drug addict and the loss of losing his girlfriend further enhanced his feelings of meaninglessness, worthlessness and low future orientation resulting in suicide.

Case Thirty-one

The deceased was a 28-year old married man from South Sikkim. He was a graduate and was in Government job. He was the only son of his parents and his family was also economically sound. Both his parents were working and living in Gangtok.

According to the friend of the deceased, his friend was very stubborn and would argue with everyone. He was good in studies because of which his parents did not say anything to him. He got a government job and also had many girl friends, but according to his friend most of these relationships did not last because he always got violent in his relationship. He always thought very highly of himself because he was good looking, played the guitar and also could sing. But most of the people would leave him, because he would become very angry and use abusive language. His married life was not good and once when his wife was pregnant he had hit her because of which she had had an abortion. After this his wife had left him. He was staying alone and would sometimes call his friend. He looked absolutely normal and no one could make out what was going on in his mind. He left a suicide note saying that *'he is confused and may be ending his life would help him find answers.'*

The narrative explains that the victim had a behavioural problem. He excelled in almost everything and this had made him over presumptuous about himself. He felt he could do and get away with anything. Being the only son he had been pampered by his parents and because of his achievements, he had always got a good deal from life. His wife left his because of domestic violence and he faced rejection for the first time in his life. This rejection and his inability to cope with it generated a conflict in his mind resulting in suicide.

Case Thirty-two

The deceased was a 38-year old, married woman, residing in East Sikkim. She studied till class V and later dropped out. She had two children. Her husband was a taxi driver owned his own taxi.

According to her husband, his was of a very cowardly nature. She would hide inside the house if there was thunder and lighting. She was also very scared of animals and once when a goat was coming towards her, she had fainted with fear. Her husband had taken her to the faith healer on several occasions and had also performed some *pujas*. Since the family was financially not very sound, she felt guilty that, the family has to waste so much of money because of her. Her husband mentioned that she could not even open a knot and always went to her children for help. She always told her husband '*I hope my children do not get the same problem like me ... everyone makes fun of me*'. Some weeks before the suicide, her husband noticed that she was not responding to things which she earlier responded to with fear. She once told him '*everyone wants to kill me, but I won't allow them to do it*'. Her daughter mentioned that, some days earlier to her suicide her mother had come to her *asking how to make a knot and she had said* 'Amma, why do you want to learn if you cannot *open* it' this had made her very angry. She left a suicide note saying that, she did not belong to this world and more people needed her in the skies.

From the narrative it can be deciphered that the victim was having a psychological problem and her inability to handle it and accept her condition added pressure to her condition. She also blamed herself for the financial losses that the family was incurring because of her sickness.

Case Thirty-three

The deceased was a 31-year old man, and a resident of West Sikkim. He was an agricultural labourer and had one son. His wife was housewife and would occasionally come to assist him in the field. He had three brothers and two sisters and they were residing in different parts of Sikkim. He dropped out of school after class VIII.

According to the wife of the deceased her husband was an introvert and also very stubborn by nature. He was an agricultural wage earner, but he did not shoulder any responsibility for his family. He drank everyday and engaged in quarrel with his wife. His wife is from Nepal and felt '*the universe conspired against me, that I landed with such a person.*' When she first met him, he posed to be very sober and caring and the moment they got married, he showed his true colours. He doubted his wife over everything and once he got drunk, he would beat her and torture her. He even doubted that his wife was having a relation with his father. He once removed all her clothes and said that '*he will have sex in front of my father; it should not trouble you since you have already slept with him*'. She was living with him in very miserable condition. When she became pregnant and delivered a baby, he did not even give her money to buy clothes, he said '*Ask the fathers to pay for the clothes*'. On the day of the suicide, he told her that now he would not drink and be nice to her and that he was going out for some time. When he returned he started hitting her again and abusing her and she realized that he was drunk again. He told her that he hated her, she ran and took shelter in the house of her neighbours that night. She told him that she had enough of him and would leave him. In the morning when she tried to open the door, she found it locked and when she peeped from the window, she saw her husband hanging from the kitchen ventilator. According to the community members, the deceased was very violent and short tempered, once he had an argument with his father and chased if with a *khukari*, the people had to intervene and he was even taken to the police station. He never mended his way and people often heard crying and wailing of his wife from his house.

The narrative highlights that the victim suffered from a behavioural psychological problem. He would physically abuse his wife and torture her. His violent nature is also reflected when he ran after his father with a *khukri*. To hide his incapacity, he had started consuming alcohol, which further worsened his problem. After getting drunk when he hit his wife, he might have become very guilty and would have realized that she was going to leave him. He realized he had reached point of no return.

Case Thirty-four

The deceased was a 29-year old man and a divorcee. He lived in his own house in Gangtok and had a small business. He was the only child of his parents. His father and mother were working in the State Government.

According to the cousin brother of the deceased he was living alone because his wife had left him some years back. His parents were living very close to his house, but not with him because he did not want to stay with them. The deceased was quite natured and generally would not share anything with his parents. He was financially well off and was living in his own house. He never told his parents about anything in his life, but whenever the topic of marriage was raised, he always mentioned that *he did not want to marry*. He was very upset after his very close friend Deepesh, got married. Deepesh stopped meeting him after he got married. He one day came and told his parents that he also wanted to marry. The parents were very happy to hear this, because he was their only child. He got married to a very pretty girl who was working as an LDC. He had invited Deepesh for the marriage but he did not come. One month after his marriage, the girl came and told his parents that she wanted to separate because something was not right and she could not tell them. His parents had asked him, but he also said that he wanted to separate from his wife. He had told his parents that marrying was the worst mistake of his life, he cannot get along with woman. It was gathered from discussion with neighbours that he was suffering from HIV, because of which he committed suicide.

This narrative may be suggesting that the victim was confused about his sexuality. He never wanted to marry and it appears that he was attracted to his friend. When his friend decided to get married, he also decided to get married but his wife may have found out and left him very soon. He may be having different sexual orientations which he could not reveal to his family members. He was suffering from HIV as mentioned by some of his neighbours.

Case Thirty-five

The deceased was a 21-year old unmarried boy and a resident of East Sikkim. He was enrolled in college but he dropped out in the middle. He had a younger brother and sister. His father was a taxi driver and he had two mothers (bigamy). He was not living with his parents, but his younger brother and sister lived with the parents.

According to the sister of the deceased, she shared very close relationship with her brother. He was a very fun loving person and was very good in singing and dancing. He had danced in many music videos and wanted to become an actor. He was also very fond of exercising and was regular at the gymnasium and had a good body. He also consumed a very good and healthy diet. However, he did not live with his parents, because, he did not share a close relation with his parents, he was very upset with his father after he married again. Although, he did not like his step mother, but he loved both his siblings, from her. He felt very sad whenever he saw his mother crying he would say *'timi na ronu... timi chod dinu'* (you should not cry, you can leave your husband). His parents would get drunk and there would be a drunken brawl every evening. This would upset him and as a result he decided to move out. One evening when he came to visit his siblings, his father and step mother started chastising him, saying that he was taking money from home and was wasting his time in singing and dancing. He also told him *"timi paise waste kardey cha, body building ma, mero paise faltu chaei na"* (you are wasting money on body building, I don't have extra money). He had walked out of the house and did not come back after that. They were informed by the police that he had hanged himself. He had left a suicide note mentioning that his family circumstances have disturbed him. He was not happy with his father getting married; he wished they could leave alcohol and live happily.

The narrative suggests that the deceased was upset with his father's second marriage. This is a case of trauma which the children face because of bigamy. He did not appreciate this and felt very sad for his mother as reflective in, when he asked his mother to leave his father. He wanted to follow his dreams, but was extremely hurt when his father said that he was wasting his money. He did not appreciate his parents drinking and all these factors had made him despondent and dejected. Disturbed relationship of his parents and family had affected him resulting in suicide.

Conclusion

From the above narratives, it can be inferred that, Suicide is, a multi-factorial phenomenon whose complexity includes, but is not limited to psychological, social,-economic, biological/psychiatric, cultural and environmental factors. All the 35 narratives that were conducted, did not point towards one reason behind committing suicide, however, from the Psycho-autopsies, after reconstruction some codes, variables and categories could be transcribed which helped us in creating indicators for analysis of the narratives. In some of the narratives, the victims have given warning signs, cries for help when they could not handle their personal problems and the social factors were going against them. They would have been saved if these signs could be picked up by their near and dear ones; some have always been on a denial mode and have camouflaged their feelings, even putting up their best behaviour so that their intentions cannot be gauged by others. There is another category in these narratives, which have just surrendered to their problems impulsively.

Individual live in psychological comfort domains, it is a type of mental conditioning and behavioural state that cause a person to create and operate in mental boundaries creating a sense of security. However, in behavioural state the person operates in an anxiety-neutral condition using a limited set of behaviour to deliver a steady level of performance usually without a sign of risk.

Individuals have high aspiration for a better life and also for spiritual growth, high expectation from their family and peer, desire for autonomy and freedom and personal factor guide the human behaviour and these factors are influenced and impacted by social structure which is very unique to every society. It is always a confluence of these factors that disturb the comfort zone. Generally, individuals try to adjust physically, psychologically and socially to get back into the comfort zone, but sometimes in their emotional state of mind they start experiencing isolation, alienation, depression and dependency along with low self-esteem, shame and guilt. Bales, 1998, has described guilt as "bothered conscience", when individual feels guilty, he feels responsible for an action that he regrets. Individual tries to justify suicide behaviour and tries to gain sympathy from society and indirectly blames related person, whom the individual perceives as a cause for their problems. This leads to low orientation tempting the individual to make an exit from all the miseries of life.

5
Conclusion

The present chapter attempts to synthesise previous chapters, to see the inter-linkage of various social factors in determining suicide in Sikkim. Suicide in Sikkim to some extent is the by-product of the contradiction between the earlier prevailing social norms and values that was characteristic feature of closed agrarian society of Sikkim in the recent past and the changing social structure in the wake of the global trend witnessed in post-nineties phase of Liberalisation, Privatisation and Globalisation. This has brought many structural changes in the socio-political and economic domain and Sikkim also could not remain isolated to this process. The intersection of these structural domains moulded the modalities of development in the State which has many socio-cultural and economic ramifications. It is theoretically established sociological fact that when society transform from simple traditional society (agrarian based economy) to the modern heterogeneous industrial society; when the society is still grappling to lift its foothold from the past but already started stepping into the future—the future driven by modernisation and globalisation, society struggles to stabilise its changing institutions, the society faces many dilemmas and in the process of this struggle, social issues and problems gradually start surfacing in all its variant forms. The liminality period of transition from one phase to another has been philosophically addressed by Thomas Kuhn in his notion of paradigm shift. These trends were also the characteristics of Europe what Karl Polanyi used the term 'period of the great transformation' to describe the massive social change which took place between 1750 and 1920 (Morrison: 2006) during the Eighteenth century, due to wave of Industrialisation and French Revolution. The massive industrialization and rise of capitalism, demographic transfer and agriculture, urbanization affected the degree of social attachment and integration to a great extent, which to Durkheimenian perspective were factors contributing to many social problems and suicide as well. These problems and emerging issues out of these transitions gave birth to sociology as a discipline.

Contextualising, this trend in the state of Sikkim, as product of the modernisation and democratisation of State followed by economic growth and its assorted consequences has brought tremendous transformation in the overall socio-economic landscape of Sikkim. Societal values can be perceived to be moving in the direction of individualism from collectivism. In such conditions individuals have witnessed and orientation towards the self and have become self-centric (husband-wife-children) and if these relations are perceived negatively, they affect the individual behaviour. The role of media and information technology, diversification in the economic activities, shift from primary to secondary and tertiary sector, growth of tourism industry, the process of urbanisation and modernisation directly or indirectly contributed to the growth of individualism, change in lifestyles, higher aspiration, competitiveness and culture of consumerism. The socio-cultural transformation often witnessed the weakening of collectivity, social ties and integration which characterised the traditional society. The transition and sudden exposure of closed traditional society with a strong sense of collective consciousness to a modern individualistic open society often have many ramifications like change in family structure, trend of nuclearisation of family, expansion of educational opportunities accompanied by outmigration from rural to urban led to so many social-cultural consequences both positive and negative. Individuals have high aspirations and desires in terms of modern life style, materialistic orientations and leisure and these aspirations influence the structural values and individual life. The emergence of individualism has given birth to various social issues, of which, suicide is one of the major social issue/problem for the society to address collectively. Therefore, the role of the state as stakeholder for maintenance of the integrity and cohesion of the society and appropriate intervention on emerging social issue like Suicide becomes utmost important. However, the problem of suicide being multi-dimensional, State cannot handle it alone. Hence, the collective role of family, civil society, NGO, educational institutions etc. become pertinent. Therefore, the chapter aims in amalgamating and integrating various causal factors by linking the empirical findings with the existing socio-cultural, economic, and political structure of the society.

Overview of the Study

Through the statistical generalisation, the study found that most of the suicide cases in the state occurred in the South district, as 34.44 per cent of the total suicide cases were found in the district. This is followed by 32.78 per cent in East district. A comparative analysis of the population ratio of each district to the rate of suicide shows that South Sikkim has the highest suicide rate. Further, it was found that suicide is high among the Sikkimese than the non-Sikkimese population, as 65.56 per cent of the suicidy have SSC/COI/*Parcha*, and the remaining 34.44 per cent did not have any of the mentioned documents. In relation to EPIC or voter ID, 80.5 per cent of the victims have voter ID, while the remaining 19.5 per cent did not. In terms of age, higher incidence of suicide is found among the 16-25 age group consisting 30.71 per cent, which is followed by the age range of 26-35 (25.73%). In the settlement pattern, 79.32 per cent of the suicide victims are from the rural population, while only 20.68 per cent constitute urban population. In relation to qualification, it was found that majority of the victims were educated up to primary (23.55%), followed by illiterate (19.42%), middle school (16.53%), and secondary and monastic education accounts for 12.81 per cent. Relatively, in terms of monthly income, majority of the deceased were found to in the income group of less than Rs. 7,500 (48.35%). Among the religious group, suicide cases were more prevalent among the Hindus.

Based on this basic information, correlation analysis was carried to link the various variables which will helped in determining the causal detrimental factor(s) that have instigated suicidal thoughts to the individuals who have acted upon it. The discussions made forward are based on the statistical interplay of various variables drawn from the 242(Z) samples and the narrative analysis carried on 350(N) samples.

Rural and Urban Difference in the Suicide

As presented in Table 3.5, the suicide percentage in the rural area is significantly higher than that of urban areas, 79.32 per cent and 20.68 per cent respectively. The rural-urban differences in the incidence of suicide can be rationalised due to simple demographic composition of rural-urban divide; as we can see that out of the total 6,10,577 population (2011 Census), 74.85 per cent of the total population resides in rural area while remaining 25.15 per cent in the urban areas. Therefore, even after statistical proportionalisation of rural-urban divide between the number of suicides and the population distribution, the study still found that the incidence of suicide is still higher in the rural areas of Sikkim, as it is observed that the incidence of suicide in the rural area is 4.47 per cent higher than the total population residing in the rural areas.

Age and Suicide

In context of age and suicide, as discussed in the previous chapter, the incidence of suicide is very high among the working population particularly those belonging to the age group of 16-45 years. As discussed in Chapter 3, Figure 3.5 that 74.28 per cent of the suicide victims belong to the age group of 16-45 years. However, if we further break up the age group, then we can see that 30.71 per cent belong to the age group of 16-25, which is highest among the categorised age groups. This is followed by those who belong to the 26-35 age group accounting 25.73 per cent of the total suicide cases. Further, in the correlation analysis between age groups, monthly income and relationship problems, we found that the specified age group, i.e. 16-45, were the most vulnerable group to suicide due to relationship problems which is further correlated with financial issues particularly with those belonging in the income raise of up to Rs. 15,000 per month. Further in the case study, 12 cases in the age group of 16-25 and nine cases in the age group of 26-35 were found to have relationship issues. However, it was also found that relationship issues were not the sole determinant in the process of the final act of suicide, social stigmatisation due to pregnancy out of wedlock (case two), cheating in examination (case 12) were found to have also contributed. Existing literatures also suggest that there are personal and structural level factors which are functioning in middle and young age group, the major studies on age and suicide show that personality disorder, alcohol dependency, anxiety disorder, depression are causes of suicide (Foster *et al.*, 1997; Lesage *et al.*, 1994). But, here we find that some structural and personal factors are functioning simultaneously and increasing the suicidal tendencies and rate like generational conflict, autonomy, freedom, life style, disturbed relationship and extra-marital affair etc. The researches on generational relations show that decreased autonomy and freedom increases dissatisfaction and negative subjective experiences in terms of stress and strain in relationship in youth (Gangrade, 1976; Kagtcibasi, 1982; Verma and Satyanarayana, 2007).

Alcoholism, Culture and State

Culturally, the consumption of alcohol is part of the Sikkimese culture and society—ritually as well as ceremoniously. Therefore, consumption of alcohol is not restricted and both socially and culturally accepted. So, to say that alcoholism was part and parcel of the society. However, suicide related cases were not evident much in the earlier times. The study shows that there is significant relation between suicide and alcohol consumption, as it is shown in Figure 3.12 that 53.53 per cent of the suicidy were habitual alcoholic, whereas, 46.47 per cent were non-alcoholic or social drinkers. Further analysis also shows that there is a positive correlation between unemployment and alcohol (62.5%), that is, unemployed population consuming alcohol are more prone to suicides than those of employed population consuming alcohol. Correlation analysis of alcohol with social isolation shows that the two are positively related as the percentage of socially isolated population consuming alcohol is higher than that of socially isolated population not consuming alcohol. This figure is marginally followed by loneliness. Income-wise, suicide is prevalent in case of lower income-holders who consume alcohol. Data analysis reveals that there is high correlation between alcoholism, unemployment/low income and suicide. Studies have found that "alcoholism and chronic use of alcohol are associated with numerous medical, psychiatric, social, and family problems.... family members, including children, exposed to a first-degree relative's alcohol problem are at risk for problems" (HB, 2013).

Several studies indicate a strong association between alcohol use and suicidal behaviours (Borges *et al.*, 2000; Conner *et al.*, 2003; Lamis *et al.*, 2010). Additionally, there is substantial evidence in prospective longitudinal research that increased alcohol consumption predicts a higher frequency of suicide ideation (Wilcox *et al.*, 2010), attempts (Robinson *et al.*, 2010). Researches on substance abuse and suicide shows that substance abuse affect the suicidal risk and anti-social behaviour, the use of alcohol and other drugs increase suicidal tendencies (Putnins, 1995; Marttunen *et al.*, 1994).

Looking at the empirical situation, narrative analysis as discussed in Chapter 4, of the cases is the evidence of the dependency on alcohol and drugs were the main reason of suicide as discussed in case 5 study. Similar is the finding of the study conducted by Henriksson and Marttunen (1993) where interpersonal events, especially partner-relationship disruptions, are most strongly associated with attempted and completed suicide in persons with alcoholism and the subjects with alcoholism experience more separations and family discord, financial trouble, and unemployment. Similar situation is found in case 5, where the triggering factors are amalgamation of alcoholism, dropout, disturb relationship and the early marriage.

Narrative Case no. 6, the deceased was a Lama (Buddhist monk) also had the problem of habitual alcoholism. He was the sole bread earner and was in debt. The isolation and loneliness after his wife's death has aggravated his mental problem and he finally committed suicide. The case also shows the combination of social and economic factors like alcoholism, low economic status which were triggering factors.

Case 8, of 46-year old divorcee woman living with her two daughters in West Sikkim, was an occasional drinker, but became a habitual drinker after her husband left her for another woman. Here the bigamy, which was traditionally and culturally legitimate practice in Sikkim among many communities and alcoholism, precipitated suicidal behaviour. The case also indicates that triggering factors are largely rooted in social structure.

Therefore, it is noticed that alcoholism which traditionally has been culturally sanctioned and has been used in rituals and ceremonious has been further strengthened by the industrialisation process, the establishment of the distilleries and breweries and the unrestricted availability of the alcohol in the State, which has contributed in the overall consumption rate of alcohol in the State.

Health and State

The saying 'A Healthy Society is a Wealthy Society' goes with the objective of human development. The growth and progress of a society solely depends on the availability of the resources—both human and natural. Health is an important component of human development. Therefore, for a healthy society, the role of the health practitioners, hospitals, and availability and accessibility of the health facilities are extremely essential. However, if we consider the health scenario of India, it has been reported that for every 1,674 people only one doctor is available. Despite the positive health indicators, the doctor-patient ratio is lower when compared with the World Health Organisation (WHO) standard norm of 1:1000 doctor-patient ratio.[1] The Sikkimese scenario is relatively worse when compared with national scenario which has been reported that for every 1,674 people one doctor is available in India. In Sikkim as per HDR 2014:2015, the State had a doctor-patient ratio of one doctor per 2,500 population which has been shown as improved to ratio of 1902, while the population-Nurse ratio is reported to be 2993 (*Sikkim Statistical Journal*, 2015). WHO report on health workforce in India claims that Sikkim has only 0.12 per cent concentration of health workers. The report stated that "states with the lowest percentage of doctors were in the north-east: Mizoram, Sikkim, Arunachal Pradesh and Nagaland". (Anand & Fan, 2016: 4). Therefore, despite the overall increase in health indicators, this is an area where state can further focus on.

As observed in the correlational analysis of health problems with monthly income that the incidence of suicide is highest among the low income group whose monthly income is less than Rs. 7,500 (42.42%), which is followed by (Rs. 15,000-25,000) income range. Therefore, those who belong to lower income group (Rs. <7,500) with health problems are prone to suicide (Ref. Chapter 4, Section on Health Problems). It is also found that stress and trauma were also correlated suggesting the need for counsellors as part of the medical and general health practices in Sikkim. During the telephonic interview with the senior psychiatrist in the STNM hospital mentioned that there are only seven practicing psychiatrists and two medical social workers in the State.[2] Empirical evidence based on the narrative analysis of the cases further suggest that the decision to take one's own life were also related to painful terminal illness from which little to no hope of reprieve exists. For instance, in the study it was found that Multi-Drug Resistant Tuberculosis (MDR-TB) patient has driven to commit suicide due to financial constraints. At the same time, it was also found that both in the interviews with doctors and the victim's family that there were cases of drug-induced psychosis related to MDR-TB led to mental instability with suicidal thoughts. In a case, where 56 years old man (Case 26) was diagnosed with MDR-TB and after he lost his daughter to the same disease this personal loss aggravated his drug-induced psychosis. This coupled with the financial drain pushed him towards suicide. Another case of a 24-year, college student (Case 21) from an affluent family who also ended her life because she could not handle the depression induced by the medication. Sometimes, it is not just economic factor, but the acceptance and belief that they will never recover from the disease that acts as a stimulator. Therefore, it becomes imperative for the state to address the question of availability and accessibility of health facilities to people from all the walks of life, and financial assistance for the needy. In the recent past, with the advancement in information and communication technology, we are able to see the emergence of cloud funding for various issues, in this respect the state can also channelized it for financially assisting those who need financial help related to health issues.

Financial Constraints, Unemployment, Substance Abuse and Suicide

In the earlier discussion, it has been pointed out that the incidence of suicide is highest among the lower income groups [Rs. <7,500 (48.35%), Rs. 7,500-15,000 (36.78%)]. It can thus be generalised that financial constraints along with other factors is also one of the major factors of suicide. The argument becomes more sensible when compared with other associable catalytic factors such as health issues, family size, alcoholism, use of tobacco, drug addiction. In relation to health and income it has been already discussed in the preceding themes. Further analysis has also found that the family size and income also plays a vital role among the low-income group, particularly to those whose family income is less than Rs. 15,000 per month with family size of 4-7 members (refer Table 3.3). Therefore, in a hilly state like Sikkim, with the prices of basic commodities out of the normal reach to the common people primarily due to high transportation charges because of hilly location and distance from Siliguri and various surcharges on the basic goods. Also, it has been observed that urban centres being the major centre for all market activities, from education to medical cares, and all other opportunities have also contributed in the hardships faced by the people.

In the narrative analysis, a 17-year old girl (Case 2), whose economic condition was in deplorable condition was in a relation with a boy, who was dumb. Besides his physical challenges, the girl was in and maintaining the relation as he was also supporting her and the family financially. However, the girl became pregnant and the boy left her. Her low economic status coupled with the fear of social stigmatisation of pre-marital pregnancy she was forced to take her life. The patriarchal social norm of stigmatisation on pre-marital sex coupled with the low economic class position and ignorance as she could adopt the family planning measures and also go for abortion, largely contributed to the suicide.

Case 6 suggests how at the time when the family is in the crisis of meeting even the basic needs becomes the victim of a contagious disease like MDR, and the extra financial burden on the family pushed the guilt ridden victim to take his own life.

Another narrative (Case 8), of a woman potter who was deserted by her husband becomes addicted to alcohol to suffice the loss of emotional support that she has gone through. Her surviving children narrated during the interview that she was aware of the meagre income and often talks about it but was never able to get out from the grasps of alcoholism. She was guilt-ridden of her state but never able to amend her behaviour, finally that driven her to commit suicide. In the statistical analysis, it was also found that alcoholism and tobacco usages were found among the low income group (Rs. <7,500); however, drug addicts were found to be higher in the income range of less than Rs. 7,500 to Rs. 25,000.

Religious Belief

Religiously speaking, as highlighted in Figure 3.8, higher occurrence of suicide was found to be amongst the Hindus (59.17%) followed by Buddhists (25.42%), Christians (12.5%), Animist (1.67%), Others (0.83%), and Islam (0.42%). However, this alone cannot establish the occurrence of suicide by religion as the same proportion also applies to the population composition of Sikkim by religious categorisation. Correlational analysis with stress reveals that among the Christians stress related suicides are high as compared to other religion. Sociologically, the possible explanation for the high suicide rate among the Hindus and Buddhist could be primarily due to lack of social cohesion and integration as argued by Durkheim in his book *Le Suicide.* The nature of social integration was found more among the Christians and they are bound to gather every Sunday in their community church bringing more social cohesion and integration. During the field visits to churches it was also found that the pastor of the church announces the achievements and rewards of each achiever in the community. This also reflects that those who have brought shame to their family or community can face severe social ostracisation. Hypothetically, it can be argued that the fear of social stigmas and shames could have be the reason why among the Christians there is high occurrence of stress related suicides.

From a pure Durkheimian interpretation religion typically acts as a protective factor against suicidal behaviour. Suicide-related beliefs, of major religions reveals some important common threads. On a macro level each of the religions reviewed is opposed to suicide. A fundamental importance is often placed on human life, and committing suicide is frequently seen as a violation of this principle. If religion does protect man from the desire to kill himself, it is not because it preaches to him respect for his person in itself, but because it is a community and binds them in collectivity. The more numerous and strong these collective states are, the more the religious community is strongly integrated; and the greater too, is its protective value. Religious group thus can provide individuals a protective factor and a level of integration necessary for uniting people with common interests and beliefs (Durkheim: 178). However, Case 18, (Ref. Chapter 4) the deceased a daughter of a *Jhakari* (Faith Healer) who was diagnosed by another faith healer, that her mood swings and depressions were because she had not transgressed to the next level of a mortal being to becoming a *Mata* (Goddess). Since, she had married (The general perception is that *Mata* is not supposed to marry), her spiritual growth had been hampered, resulting in her unstable mental condition. Her religious aspirations and the flux in her mind that she had wronged the order of the divine, compelled her to take her life. Case 19 of another faith healer, this time a man, belonging to the Limboo community aspiring to be a *Bijwa* (Faith healer of Limboo Community) reveals that his aspirations and desires to see himself as a revered *Bijwa* was putting stress and expectations on his mind. His statement that *sano sano phuk phak, hamroo bao kasto gyane thiyo* (I do minor shamanistic rituals, forwarding spirits, my father was such a great shaman) talks about his spiritual craving and also his aspirations to succeed.

With the creeping of modern so called rational values, the shamanistic practices, and belief that girls and boys get the divine power and becomes *mata/Bijwa* etc., which were very strong in traditional society comes in conflict with the values of modern society where, modern education and professional degrees etc. has high priority of every individual. As such with the introduction of medical science accompanied by the rising awareness among the common people, the belief on traditional shamans/*matas* etc. as faith healer having divine possession has been shaken somehow, which also affected the means of earning and subsistence of these people, a feature in traditional society. The contradiction between these two values, therefore, could have further contributed to the dilemmas and stress on the individual.

Education, Dropout and Unemployment

Education plays a vital role in the social growth and progress of society. Rousseau in his work *Emily: Or on Education* (1762) pointed out that education played an important role in the development of man as a rational being. Relatively to the argument pointed by Rousseau, if we refer to Table 3.6 of Chapter 3 on the educational qualifications of the suicide victims, it is observed that majority of the suicide victims (23.55%) were educated up to the primary level only, which is being followed by those who have never been into any kind of formal educational system (19.42%), next to it is up to middle-school educated accounting 16.53 per cent, and so on. Therefore, most of the suicide cases occurred among those who are illiterate, primary to higher secondary educated, and also those who have done monastic education, those suicidy who belong to these range constitute 93.80 per cent of the total suicides. It was also found that 172 (in absolute number) or 72.57 per cent of the deceased were dropouts. The study suggests that majority of the suicidy were less educated and dropouts. Occupation-wise, it was found in the correlation analysis that higher cases of suicides were common among the dropouts who were occupationally engaged in farming (36.63%), followed by housewives (16.28%), unemployed (8.72%) and so forth. Therefore, there seems to be an inverse relationship between educational level of the suicide victim and the frequency of suicide.

As discussed in Chapter 2, the overall literacy rate of Sikkim as per 2011 Census is 81.4 per cent, which is far better than All India literacy rate of 74.04 per cent. In terms of Gross Enrolment Ratio (GRE) Sikkim is still better than the All India ratio. For instance, the GER at primary level in Sikkim in 2013-14 was 124.4 per cent whereas All India was 101.4 per cent, giving Sikkim an edge of 23 per cent ahead of All India ratio. However, in terms of Net Enrolment Ratio (NER), Sikkim suffer a major setback, as Sikkim's NER (83.5%) is 4.6 per cent lesser than All India NER of 88.1 per cent at the primary level. Even at the upper primary level the NER of Sikkim worsens as compared to All India NER of 70.2 per cent, Sikkim's NER at this level was 59.9 per cent which is 10.3 per cent lower than the All India NER in 2013-14. Therefore, Low NER suggests either the accumulation of overage children in primary level or dropout in Sikkim which can be an area of concern which the State needs to address, keeping the repercussion and emerging social ills of the Sikkim emanating out from the dropouts. Education is not just about providing the means of livelihood but it also to become a rational thinker, as suggested by Rousseau, to appropriate their knowledge in developing the coping mechanism in stressful situations enabling them to handle the problems of life efficiently rather than succumbing in it and forcing one to take her/his own life. For instance, dropout, unemployment, and failure in relationship was evident in cases 5 and 7. The above highlighted argument is also supported in other studies (Charles & Rudolf, 1987; Tuncay *et al.*, 2008) pointing out that individuals with higher educations have better coping strategy, i.e. problem focused coping, positive refraining, active coping, religion and instrumental supports, which acts as an impediment to committing suicide.

Marital Status and Suicide

Suicides related to marital status is one of the most thought-provoking factors in the present study. As highlighted in Figure 3.10, it is observed that suicide in Sikkim is highest among the married individuals constituting 58.51 per cent of the total suicide cases in Sikkim. This is an important aspect of the study as in most of the suicide cases observed around the world are common among the unmarried individuals. Durkheim's (1897) study also supported that married individuals are less prone to commit suicide than unmarried individuals. Durkheim believed that after 20, an individual enjoys a 'coefficient of preservation'. However, in our study more married individuals had committed suicide demonstrating the fact that conjugal society does not promise immunity against suicide. Similar findings were also supported by Velasco and Mynko (1973). In the narrative analysis, represented in Cases 11 and 17 found that relationship problems related to adultery on the part of the husbands were coming out more prominently in the study. On the other hand, alcoholism and illness were also found which create relationships problems as analysed in Case 20.

Gender and Suicide

In overall, gender data representation reflects equal representation of both male and female with 50 per cent each among those who committed suicides; however, district-wise analysis presents difference in the gender ratio of incidence of suicide, observable in Figure 3.1. In relation to gender differences, studies have suggested that women tend to engaged more in suicidal behaviour resulting in injury or a non-fatal outcome. In 1998, researchers Silvia Sara Canetto and Isaac Sakinofsky called it as 'gender paradox of suicidal behaviour'. Studies carried out in India also shows similar trend. In relation to which, studies have suggested that men are socially reared to be more alone and independent, and to have more difficulty seeking help when in distress. Others still suggest that the coping conditions and styles of men are more aligned to fighting, violence, anger and modification by acute substance abuse. Gopalakrishna (1978) and Rao (1972) also in a study conducted in union territory of Goa, found that there were more male suicides than females.

Changes in Family Relations and Suicide

Sikkim, although small state both demographically as well as geographically, yet it is not far aloof from the impact of the changing global '-scapes' (Appadurai's concepts of five-scapes that propagated in global exchange of ideas and information). In Sikkim, the economy driven 'Financescapes', information driven 'Mediascapes', and technology driven 'Technoscapes' played a significant role in changing the socio-cultural and economic fabrics of the Sikkimese society. The changing 'scapes' of the society has brought tremendous transformation in the rural areas of the Sikkim, as we have already seen the its impact in the form of high rate of suicide in the rural areas of Sikkim. This has brought change in the rural economy as well as in the family structure of the rural society of the state. The transformation from the self-sufficient rural economy to the dependent economy to urban centres has created the pull factor to urban centres, at the same time the social status assigned to farming as an occupation has also generated the push factor from the agrarian economy to service sectors. Due to which, more people from the rural areas are forced to migrate in search for better prospects and respectable jobs. This is also reflected in occupational shift reflected in 2011 Census, when compared to 1991 Census and diversification of economy. In turn, this tremendously impacted the composition and structure of family, transforming from joint to nuclear family, further giving birth to individualism rather than collectivism, as evident in the Cases 2 and 5 of the narrative analysis.

Acculturation Stresses Due to Globalisation

In India, study by L. Vijaykumar (2007) highlighted that Development has led to an increase in mental health problems. Liberalisation of the economy and privatisation results in increased income disparities, there is a change in the family structure and individuals are not able to meet role obligations, this has resulted in increased stress and difficulty in adjusting to the new norms and values associated with modernization. Similarly, *In Suicide: A Paradox of Development in Kerala,* Halliburton (1998) mentions that Kerala also has a high rate of suicide despite achievements in health, education and social welfare high-literacy and an impressive record of socio-economic development. A large epidemiological study in India (Patel, V., 2012) found higher rates of youth suicide occurring among the educated *versus* illiterate population. "Suicide death rates were greater in the richer states (many of which are in the South) and among those with higher levels of education. In contrast, suicide death rates are greater among the less educated in high-income countries" (Patel, V., 2012: 9). Development can result is weakening of family bonds, more intergenerational and family conflict, decrease in social cohesion, loss of traditional means of livelihood and economic activity, unable to obtain English language skills and other skills necessary to compete for employment in the modern marketplace, there is also Cultural confusion with rapid social change where traditional norms, values and lifestyles are being replaced by consumer culture values, norms and lifestyles. Sikkim as a state of India, has opened-up to economic development in recent years with investment in infrastructure and communications technology resulting in rapid social change, which can have a destabilizing impact on the society. It was a harmonious agriculturally based religious society based on social cohesiveness and mechanical solidarity. However, development is bringing about social and cultural changes through increasing media exposure to the global consumer economy (Jaipal and Sachdeva, 2017, unpublished). Rapid cultural change and erosion of indigenous cultural values and identity through the increasing inter-connectedness that globalization brings with it, seem to be at the root of pervasive feelings of stress and anxiety.

Summing up both quantitative and qualitative narrative analysis, it can be safely concluded that most of the causative factors of suicide are rooted largely on social structure. Although, subjective experience varies across individual, nonetheless, these forms a pattern and shared as inter-subjective experience by many of the victims. The cases of diverse nature ranging from emotional, psychological, and relational directly or indirectly are largely rooted in changing socio-cultural and economic structure of the State.

Notes

1. Reported in the *Hindustan Times* published on 1st of September, 2016, titled 'Healthcare crisis: Short of 5 lakh doctors, India has just 1 for 1,674 people'.
2. Interview conducted on 15th of September, 2017.

6

Grassroots Perspective and Recommendations

Drawing from the previous chapters on the discussion of various determinants and causes of suicide, the present chapter attempts to make recommendation which is context and cultural specific to Sikkim. However, before we proceed to recommendations, it is important to highlight how the society perceives suicide. This has come out of the group discussions which were done in the Pakyong, Yangyang and Magan and Geysing. These discussions were attended by teachers, panchayat members, NGO workers, officials from the state administration at sub-divisional level and members from the civil society. The chapter is divided into two sections—Section A represents the perspective of suicide at the grassroots level, i.e. how the local bodies of community perceive about suicide. Whereas, Section B includes the recommendations which are based on the empirical findings and stakeholders perception.

SECTION A

Societal Perception of Suicide

- The readily available information especially through Facebook, Whatsapp, and other sources and the unrestricted accessibility to numerous information and reports about suicide through various social media has impacted the young minds of the teens and young adults. A general trend is observable that the young minds are interpreting suicide as an ultimate solution to all woes of life.
- There is a general belief across all religions and communities that evil spirits locally referred as '*siyey*' is responsible for

all social evils in the society. As society becomes more secular and modern, people are no longer believing in such superstitions. Therefore, they suggested that religious practices and values should be imbibed; in absence of appeasement of deities or *devi-devta* and due to spirit possession and black magic, suicide is the result.

- In relation to mental illness, most of the people in the village take the help of traditional healers rather than seeking the help of professional mental health practitioners resulting in worsening the person's psychological condition.
- Change in the family size structure basically the nuclearization of family structure has also contributed to suicide to an extent, as traditionally rural society used to have large family size where children were looked after by kin and siblings. The disintegration of joint and extended family resulted in lack of emotional and social support of the children. However, the discussions in North district highlighted that the social fabric is still intact which explains relatively less percentage of suicide in North Sikkim.
- There was a consensus among all participants that present generation lacks the capacity to struggle or coping mechanism and are used to easy life. Instead of quality time with kids, the parents provide all their financial needs and supports hence are they not able to handle the real-life situations.
- The transformation in the ICT has made the children more dependent on the virtual world with 'the phone as their best friend' looping away from the real world, making them socially isolated and self-centric.
- Sikkimese youth are making achievements in education, while the local economy has not been able to provide commensurate employment, resulting in a population of 'educated unemployed' often leading to increasing the frustration levels among them.
- Due to economic deprivation among a section, despite performing well at school level, they are not being able to send their kids for higher education. They eventually settle for non-lucrative jobs and this brings discontent in them.
- There was consensus among members of civil society members in South Sikkim the social environment at home,

broken families, alcoholism, bigamy and extra martial affairs largely contribute to suicidal behaviour.

- These days' teenagers are also confused about their sexuality, a case was highlighted of a girl, in which she committed suicide after her best friend was married to someone else. In a transitional society like Sikkim, confused sexual orientation is not yet discussed openly.
- The high expectation and unrealistic expectation from life, particularly the teenagers often results in sense of rejection. A reported case in North Sikkim, of a school student, who hanged himself when his parents refuse to provide a PSP (video game).
- The group discussion also came to the consensus that many suicidal cases were related to chronic illness like MDR-TB, cancer, epilepsy etc. and the economic burden they put to family, which was also found in empirical evidence.
- A member from an NGO in Gangtok while expressing his view on alcoholism and drug addiction, mentioned 'that there is an urgent need to address the evils of discrimination and stigmatization against the drug abusers. A simple act of humanity can sometimes be sufficient in saving a life.
- Increasing class differences, social inequality, and consumerism also results in constant comparisons, competition, generating stress and negativity with a sense of relative deprivation putting undue stress on the individuals, which is also a current trend in Sikkim. This was also opined by Principal, Yangang Senior Secondary School, Mr. A.D. Chettri and teachers. They further pointed out that *materialism and individualism has increased and values and spirituality have taken a back seat resulting in* breakdown of individual's morality. *Similar opinion was given by* Psychologist at STNM hospital.

Summing up the discussion, it largely points to the core structural reasons. The members of the Society felt the factors responsible for suicide are: integration of the individual with institutions like family, economic, religion and culture needs to be comprehended more systematically. Secondly, feelings of degradation of status, disintegration of joint household and dropout of the children from schools needs attention. Thirdly, the problem of Alcoholism and Drug abuse along with diseases like MDR-TB, epilepsy needs to be looked at in order to comprehend this phenomenon. Fourthly, contemporary competitive environment, in all the walks of life, such as the current modalities of development, globalisation, the rise in the use of internet and other ICTs etc. which are inducing stress in the general population, needs to be studied.

SECTION B

Based on the empirical findings of 242 quantitative and 35 qualitative samples and group discussions, following suggestions are recommended:

Family and Educational Institution

Family

- There should be positive parenting and parent's involvement in the progress of their child as well as his/her problems an involved in dealing with adolescence problems and stress. There should be proper parent teacher co-ordination and parents need to be encouraged to attend annual functions or parents teachers meeting, so that the child feels cared for.
- Parents need to be counselled that meeting the material needs of the child is one aspect of parenting, but they need to spend quality time with their children. They should be aware of the events going on in their child's life, their friends, things which are stressing them etc. It can begin with a simple question 'What happened today at school'.
- Parents need to be friends to their children, so that they can share their feelings and problems with them without fear and hesitation. Children have unrealistic expectations from life and somehow when they do not receive the support from their parents, it can create a big void in their life. Parents should talk to their children about physical intimacies, good touch-bad touch, menstrual issues, relationships etc.
- Children from broken home and single parenting child should be handled cautiously and carefully as they have been deprived of channelizing their emotions and expressions which in future could be easily vulnerable to drugs and

suicide. Examples of such cases are plenty in Sikkim. Single parents need to take extra caution regarding this factor.

Educational Institution

- Every institutional head should be proactive in sensitising teaching fraternity in taking care of the problems faced by pupils at school. For example a child from broken family can have serious emotional disorders which hinder them to keep up with normal mainstream stereotypical growth, hence should be handled sensitively, however, profiling of such children should not be made public and its confidentiality should be maintained.
- A counselling cell should be opened at every school and teachers who are sensitive and apathetic to the needs and problems of the children can be hired or trained as a counsellor. They can be given a preliminary training and some remuneration for the extra efforts as an incentive.
- Every class teacher should also be trained to be sensitive to the needs of the students. In today's age of information and technology online counselling is also not a bad option, provided monitored either by school or parents.
- Values Education, Coping and Life Skills Education can be imparted at school level at school's initiatives.
- Yoga and relaxation therapy, taekwondo, extra-curricular activities, outdoor games should be introduced in every school. Both parents and teachers should motivate the children to participate in these activities.
- Sex education/adolescent education should be introduced, it may not be a part of curriculum but teachers should not hesitate to talk about it. In this age of internet, children already have access to a lot of information; it was always advisable to give unfiltered information to children.
- Sensitisation programme on Drug use and Alcohol dependence, HIV/AIDS need to be initiated to educate about their negative health effects.
- School managing committee which includes the principals, parents, teachers and panchayat members could function as the coordinating committee at village level to take initiatives.

Intervention from Civil Society and Panchayat

- Panchayat can sensitise members of civil society and assist in condemning of stigmatization that the victim's family faces after the act. Instead, there is a need for airing collective grief for suicide victims. There can be some listening circles, where individuals can sit together and share stories.
- The panchayat members can identify community volunteers who could be the ward panchayat representative for each ward of a GPU, who would be willing to help in emergencies and make referrals to PHC doctors, or identify community members who could take on that task.
- The panchayat members in their meeting should talk about general social issues like drugs, alcohol, bigamy, tuberculosis and mental health.
- The panchayat should assist in starting 24 hour suicide help lines in their respective gram panchayat units GPU.
- Skits could be produced by civil society at Panchayat initiatives in coordination with National School of Drama. Community involvement and sensitisation could be initiated through food festivals, pamphlets. Suicide signs with catchy messages could be written in a more engaging manner, e.g. writing in the form of Nepali poetry.
- Panchayat should work with indigenous faith healers, train them in counselling and develop ways to integrate modern science with traditional beliefs, so that core beliefs that are fear based and ineffective can be removed while traditional beliefs that promote Mental Health and well-being are strengthened.

Religion

- Individuals should be encouraged to participate in religious or other allied activities in order to instill a sense of belonging with the community and strengthening social ties.
- In relation to religious festivals emphasis should be given to the essence about the festival rather than the glamour aspect of the festival, which sometimes puts unnecessary economic burden on the individuals increasing level of stress.

- Rituals associated with rites of passage should be simplified so that the family is not financially pressed.
- Faith healers should be sensitised not create fear in mind of the individuals who approach them for treatment and direct them to doctors, if they are unable to solve the problem.

Medical Doctors

- The State faces a shortage of human resources; regular and professional trainers should come back and train other people in a short term course.
- More clinical psychologists, psychiatrists are needed in government hospitals as well as private. Many doctors themselves are deprived of psychological training; a basic fundamental psychological training should be given to them. There is a need to creating a good and cooperative relation between psychiatrists and psychologists.
- There should be candid relationship between ASHA to Anganwadis to Panchayats to local administrative bodies to that of a doctor, so that the problem of mental stress and illness could be discovered and interventions made at the appropriate time before it is too late.
- The drugs administered for Tuberculosis and MDR-TB have a side effect that it induces psychosis, so such patients from the inception of the treatment should be treated carefully and sensitively.

Media

- Media can initiate sensitive awareness campaigns.
- Sharing of motivational and success stories will be of help on Social media.

NGOs

- Sensitising the public through the distribution of pamphlets, papers, literature and through technological assistance. Focus on creating innovative new writings, slogans and pamphlets.
- Creating a network of various NGOs so that experiences can be shared easily and on doing that we will lessen the gap of communication.

- Every NGO should responsibly share success stories so that it inspires people and prevent others from such a heinous act. Personal experiences of suicide survival victims will influence and play a vital role.
- Using of social networking intelligently and properly, opening of new Whatsapp and new Facebook page which is accessible to the general public can be started and everyday an inspirational quotation can be posted.

State

- Establish a Coordinating Committee of stakeholders from the Department of Health and Family Welfare, Sikkim University, Doctors, NGOs, Panchayat and Teachers.
- Health registry maintained by the PHC/PHSC and nurses in each village can have a column added to it on Mental Health. This can serve as a monitoring system of Mental Health and early warning sign of suicide risk.
- The state should also initiate cloud funding for those individuals who need financial assistance.
- Value Education training modules for children to be developed in the school system and to be incorporated in the curriculum at elementary level, where Human Resource Development Department, Government of Sikkim can play a vital role. This was also suggested by the civil society members, teachers and parents during group discussion.
- Health Ministry of the State and Educational Head should work collaboratively over the issues of mental health and stress as well as emotional disorders at regular intervals during each academic session.

Strengthen Existing Programmes

- The dynamic initiatives and programmes being undertaken by PHCs and doctors in district hospitals under the Health Ministry (Dr. Gurung and Dr. Satish Rasaily) are holistic and approach the problem at multiple levels. This must be strengthened and sustained and these models could be used in all the districts and percolated down to the GPU level.

- Vocational training should be provided for unemployed addicts to give those alternative opportunities and wean them away from their dependence, efforts in this direction are already under way by Kishore Sharma, *Manav Jeevan Sudhar Evam Manav Kshamata Nirman*, Soreng, West Sikkim.
- The SAATHI (Sikkim Against Addiction Towards Healthy India) programme, was started by the Hon'ble M.P. Shri P.D. Rai is very successful at the school level in which school children are used as mediators between their peers and the school administration, so that their problems of substance abuse can be addressed. Similar Gatekeeper training programme can also be implemented for suicide at the community level volunteers, who can be used as a gate keeper in identifying the warning signs and taking steps accordingly.
- 24 hour Suicide Crisis Hotline started by Mr. K.C. Nima at STNM Hospital is a welcome step and should be taken forward.

Summing up, the study, there is a need for short-term and long term culturally sensitive interventions at many levels. There is an urgent need to support and strengthen the initiatives that are already under way. The anticipated solution lies in the successful discourse between internal actors, viz. family, close relatives, friends and the external actors like teachers, Panchayat etc. The State as an external agency can play a vital role in addressing socio-economic issues that are largely rooted in social structure.

References

Abramson, L.Y., Metalsky, G.J. and Alloy, L.B. (1989). "Hopelessness depression: A theory based subtype of depression", *Psychological Review*. 96 (2): 358 372.

Alfred, A. (1972). *The Savage God: A Study of Suicide*. Bloomsbury Publishing.

Anand, Sudhir and Victoria Fan. (2016). *The Health Workforce in India: Human Resources for Health Observer Series No. 16*. Geneva: WHO.

Assadi, M. (1998). "Farmers' Suicides: Signs of Distress in Rural Economy", *Economic and Political Weekly*, Vol. 33(14): 747-48.

Bales, N. (1998). "Coping with Shame and Guilt." http://fbg-church.org/articles/guilt.htm

Baumeister, R.F. (1990). "Suicide as escape from self", *Psychological Review*. 90-113.

Bilton, T. (1996). *Introductory Sociology*, Basingstoke: Macmillan Press.

Black, S.T. (1993). "Comparing genuine and stimulated suicide notes: A new perspective". *Journal of Counseling and Clinical Psychology*, 61(4): 699-702.

Borges, G.; Walters, E.E. and Kessler, R.C. (2000). "Associations of substance use, abuse and dependence with subsequent suicidal behaviour", *American Journal of Epidemiology*, 151, 781-789.

Bouckoms, A. and Streiner, D. (1982). "Parental Loss and Family Stability in Attempted Suicide", *Arch Gen Psychiatry*, 39(9): 1081-1085.

Bruner, J., (1990). *Acts of Meaning*, Cambridge. Harvard University Press.

Charles, J.H. and Rudolf, H.M. (1987). "Personal and contextual determinants of coping strategy", *Journal of Personality and Social Psychology*, 52(5): 946-955.

Chettri, R., Gurung, J. and Singh, B. (2016). "A 10-year retrospective study of Suicide in Sikkim, India: A Socio-demographic Profile and risk assessment", *Indian Journal of Psychiatry*, Vol. 58(4) Octobêr-December.

Conner, K.; Li, Y.; Meldrum, S.; Duberstein, P. and Conwell, Y. (2003). "The role of drinking in suicidal ideation: Analyses of Project MATCH data", *Journal of Studies on Alcohol*, 64, 402-408.

Deshpande, R.S. (2002). "Suicide by Farmers in Karnataka: Agrarian Distress and Possible Alleviatory Steps", *Economic and Political Weekly*, Vol. 37(25): 2601-10.

Durkheim, E. (1979). *Suicide: A study in Sociology, (translation)*. By John, A. Spaulding and George Simpson (New York: Free Press). (Originally published in 1897).

Fleer, J. and Pasewark, R.A. (1982). "Prior public health agency contacts of individuals committing suicide", *Psychological Review*, 50 (3, Pt.2), 1319-1324.

Freud, S. (1920). *A general introduction to psycho-analysis*, New York: Boni and Liveright.

Freud, S. (1936). *The basic writings of Sigmund Freud* (A.A. Brill, Ed. And Trans). New York. Original work published in 1940.

Futterman, S. (1961). *Suicide,* In Norman, L. Farberow and Edwin.

Geertz, C. (1973). *The Interpretation of Cultures: Selected Essays*, New York: Basic.

Gibbs, J.P. and Martin, W.T. (1964). *Status Integration and Suicide: A Sociological Study*, Eugene, Oregon: University of Oregon Press.

Goldthorpe, J.H. (2001). "Causation, Statistics and Sociology", *European Sociological Review,* 17(1): 1-20.

Halbwachs, M. (1930). *Les Causes du Suicide*, Paris: Felix Alcan.

Hawton, K.; Houston, K.; Malmberg, A. and Simkin, S. (2003). "Psychological autopsy interviews in suicide research: The reactions of informants", *Archives of Suicide Research*, 7: 73-82.

HDR, 2014 (2015), Routledge.

Henriksson, M.M.; Aro, H.M., Marttunen, M.J. *et al* (1993). "Mental disorders and co-morbidity in suicide", *American Journal of Psychiatry*; 150: 935-940.

Iyer, K.G. and M.S. Manik (2000). *Indebtedness, Impoverishment and Suicides in Rural Punjab*, Delhi: Indian Publishers and Distributors.

Jacobs, D. and Klein, M.E. (1993). "The Expanding role of psychological autopsies", In A.A. Leenars (Ed.), *Suicidology.* Northvale, NJ. Jason Aronson.

Jaipal, R. and Sachdeva, S.A. (2016). *Social and Psychological Costs of Development for Youth in Sikkim*. (Unpublished).

Jalles, J.T. and Andresen, M.A. (2015). "The Social and Economic Determinants of Suicide in Canadian Provinces", *Health Economics Review,* 5(1): 1-12.

Jodhka, S. (2006). "Beyond Crises: Rethinking Contemporary Punjab Agriculture", *Economic and Political Weekly*, Vol. 16(4): 1530-1537.

Kalingman, A. and Hocdorf, Z. (1993). "Coping with distress and self harm: The Impact of Primary Preventation Programme away Adolescents", *Journal of Adolescence*, 16: 121-140.

Kessler, R.; Berglund, P.; Borges, G.; Nock, M. and Wang, P. (2005). "Trends in suicide ideation, Linking anti-social behaviour, substance use and personality: An integrative quantitative model of the adult externalizing spectrum", *Journal of Abnormal Psychology*, 116: 645-666.

Koskay, R.; Sitourn, S. and Zubrick, S. (1990). "Are adolescents who have suicidal thoughts, different from those who attempt suicide?" *Journal of Nervous and Mental Disease*, 178: 38-43.

Kumar, U., Mandal, M.K. (Ed.) (2010). *Suicidal Behaviour: Assessment of People-at-Risk*, New Delhi: Sage.

Kumar, P. and Sharma, S.L. (1998). *Suicides in Rural Punjab,* Institute for Development and Communication, Chandigarh.

Lachungpa, P. (2010). *Monastic Education in Sikkim*, Unpublished M.A. Dissertation.

Lamis, D.A. and Malone, P.S. (2011). "Alcohol-related problems and risk of suicide among college students: The mediating roles of belongingness and burdensomeness", *Suicide and Life Threatening Behaviour*, 41: 543-553.

Leenaars, A.A. (1989). "Suicide across the adult life-span: An archival study", *Crisis*, 10: 132-151.

Mann, J.J.; A. Apter, J. Bertolote, A. Beautrais, D. Currier, A. Hass *et al.* (2005). "Suicide Prevention Strategies: A Systematic Review", *Journal of American Medical Association*, 294 (16): 2064-74.

Marttunen, M.; Aro, H.; Henriksson, M. and Lonnquist, J.K. (1994). "Psychosocial stressors more common in adolescent suicide with alcohol abuse compared with depressive adolescent suicide." *Journal of American Academy of Child and Adolescent Psychiatry*, 33: 490-497.

Marwaha, S. (2005). "How best to tackle the problem of suicide", *The Tribune*, Chandigarh, 25 June.

Menninger, K. (1938). *Man against himself.* New York: Harcourt, Brace & world.

Mills, C.W. (2000). *Sociological Imagination*, New York: Oxford University Press.

Mishra, S. (2006). "Suicides of Farmers in Maharashtra", Report Submitted to the Government of Maharashtra, IGIDR Mumbai. http://www.igidr.ac.in/suicide/suicide.htm. (accessed 8th June 2016).

Mohanakumar, S. and Sharma, R.K. (2006). "Analyses of Farmer Suicides in Kerala", *EPW,* XLI (16): 1553-58.

Mohanty, B.B. (2005). "We are Like the Living Dead: Farmer Suicides in Maharashtra", *Journal of Peasant Studies,* 32(2): 243-76.

Morrison, K. (2006). *Marx, Durkheim, Weber: Formations of Modern Social Thought*, New Delhi: Sage Publications.

Moss, H.B. (2013). "The impact of alcohol on society: a brief overview", *Soc. Work Public Health*; 28(3-4):175-7.

Movement against State Repression (1998). Cited in Singh, J. (Ed.) Suicide in Rural Punjab, Monograph series IV. *Journal of Child and Adolescent Psychiatry*, 33: 490-497.

Nakane, C. (1966). "A Plural Society in Sikkim: A Study of the Interrelations of Lepchas, Bhutias and Nepales", In C. Von Furer Heimendorf (Ed.), *Caste and Kin in Nepal, India and Ceylon*. Bombay: Asia Publishing House.

Narasimha Rao, P. and Suri, K.C. (2006). "Dimensions of Agrarian Distress in Andhra Pradesh", *EPW,* XLI (16): 1546-52.

NCRB (2015). *Accidental Deaths and Suicides in India 2014.* New Delhi: Ministry of Home Affairs, Government of India.

NCRB (2016). *Accidental Deaths and Suicides in India 2015.* New Delhi: Ministry of Home Affairs, Government of India.

Nisbet, A.R. (1965). *Emile Durkheim.* New Jersey: Englewood Cliffs, Prentice Hall.

Patel, V.; Ramasundarahettige, C.; Vijayakumar, L.; Thakur, J.S.; Gajalakshmi, V., Gururaj, G. *et al.* (2012). "Suicide mortality in India: A nationally representative survey", *Lancet*; 379: 2343-51.

Paykel, E.S. (1991). "Depression in women", *British Journal of Psychiatry.* 158 (10), 22-29. *Personal Relationships, 7,* 495-506.

Peterson, S.; Baeyer, V.; Metalsky, A. and Seligman, (1982). "Attributional Style Questionnaire in Robinson", J.P., Shaver, P.R. and Wrightsman, L.S. (Ed.) *Measures of Personality and Social Psychological Attitudes,* Vol. (1) Measures of Psychological Attitudes Series. Academic Press.

Putnins, A.L. (1995). "Recent drug use and suicidal behaviour among young offenders", *Drug and Alcohol Review*, 14, 151-158.

Registrar General of India 2012.

Revathi, E. (1998). "Farmers' Suicides: Missing Issues", *Economic and Political Weekly.* May 16, 1998.

Robinson, J.; Harris, M.; Harrigan, S.; Henry, L.; Farrelly, S., Prosser, A., *et al.* (2010). "Suicide attempt in first-episode psychosis: A 7.4 year follow-up study", *Schizophrenia Research*, 116, 1-8.

S. Shneidman (Ed.). *The Cry for Help,* New York: McGraw-Hill.

Schreiber, R.S. (2001). "The 'How to' of grounded theory: Avoiding the pitfalls", In R.S. Schreiber and P.N. Stern (Eds.) *Using grounded theory in nursing* (pp. 56-84). New York: Springer Publishing.

Shiva, V. and Afsar, H.J. (1998). *Stronger than Steel: Peoples Movement against Globalisation and the Gopalpur Steel Plant,* New Delhi: Research Foundation for Science, Technology and Ecology.

Shneidman, E. (1993). *Suicide as Psychache: A Clinical Approach to Self Destructive Behaviour*, London: Jason Aronson Inc.

Shridhar, V. (2006). "Why do Farmers Commit Suicide?: The case of Andhra Pradesh", *Economical and Political Weekly*, XLI(16): 1559-1565.

Singh, K.S. (1993). *Sikkim,* Volume XXXIX, Anthropological Survey of India, Calcutta: Seagull Books.

Sinsbury, P. (1956). *Suicide in London: An Ecological Study*, New York: Basic Books.

Stekel, W. (1910). "Symposium on suicide", In Friedma, P. (Ed.). *On Suicide.* New York: International Universities Press, 1977, pp. 33-141

Sudhir, A. and Victoria, F. (2016). *The Health Workforce in India: Human Resources for Health Observer Series No. 16.* Geneva: WHO.

Thapa, S. (2002). *Ethnicity, Class and Politics of Sikkim,* Ph.D. Thesis (Unpublished), Department of Sociology and Social Anthropology, North Bengal University.

Thapa, S. (2009). "Women in Sikkim in Changing Perspective", In Lal Neihzovi (Ed.) *Changing Status of Women in NE States*; New Delhi: Mittal Publications.

Thapa, S. (2012). "Resource Distribution and Ethnic Reproduction: A Study in Sikkim", In Samhita Choudhari and D.C. Roy (ed.) *Resource Management: Human and Natural Perspective on NE Region*, Kolkata: Readers Service.

Thapa, S. and Lhasungpa, N. (2013). "Gender and Social Issues", Background Paper submitted for Human Development Report, 2014.

Torill, M. (2006). "Reflections on the Narrative Research Approach", *International Journal of Qualitative Method*. 5(4).

Tuncay, T.; Musbak, I.; Gok, D.E. and Kuttu, M. (2008). "The relationship between anxiety, coping strategies and characteristic of patients with diabetes", *Health and Quality of Life Outcome*. http://www.hglo.com/content/6/1/79

Vasavi, A.R. (1999). "Agrarian Distress in Bidar: Market, State and Suicides", *Economic and Political Weekly*, 34(32): 2263-68.

Velasco, J.R. and Mynko, L. (1973). "Suicide and Marital Status: A Changing Relationship?", *Journal of Marriage and Family*, Vol. 35, No. 2, Special Sections: Moving and the Wife, Women in Latin America), pp. 239-244.

Verma, S. and Sachdeva, S.A. (2013). "Suicide among Sikkim Youth: An Exploration. Shoryabhumi", Vol. 1(1) February-April.

Verma, S. and Sachdeva, S.A. (2014). "Culture, Social Process and Suicide: A Qualitative Enquiry", In *Social Psychology of Health: The Issues and Concerns*, Urmi Nanda Biswas (ed.), New Delhi. Concept Publishing Company Pvt. Ltd.

Verma, S.K. and Satyanarayana, A. (2007). "Influencing Factors of Intergenerational relations in Indian Family: A Narrative Approach", *Journal of Research and Development*, Help Age India.

Vijaykumar, L. (2007). "Suicide and its presentation: The urgent need in India", *Indian Journal of Psychiatry*. April-June; 49(2): 8184.

Werlanga, B.G. and Botegab, N.J. (2003). "A semi-structured interview for psychological autopsy in suicide cases", *Rev Bras Psiquiatr* 25(4):212-9.

WHO (2016). *Preventing Suicide: A Community Engagement Toolkit*, Geneva: WHO.

WHO (2014). *Preventing Suicide: a Global Imperative*. World Health Organization.

Wilcox, H.; Conner, K. and Caine, E. (2004). "Association of alcohol and drug use disorders and completed suicide: An empirical review of cohort studies", *Drug and Alcohol Dependence*, 76, S11-S19.

Index